GO HOME OR DIE HERE

GO HOME OR DIE HERE

VIOLENCE, XENOPHOBIA AND THE REINVENTION OF DIFFERENCE IN SOUTH AFRICA

EDITED BY SHIREEN HASSIM, TAWANA KUPE AND ERIC WORBY
PHOTOGRAPHS BY ALON SKUY
FOREWORD BY BISHOP PAUL VERRYN

WITS UNIVERSITY PRESS

Wits University Press

1 Jan Smuts Avenue

Johannesburg, South Africa

http://witspress.wits.ac.za

© Text 2008: Individual contributors

© Photographs 2008: Alon Skuy

First published 2008

ISBN 978-1-86814-487-7

Cover photograph by Alon Skuy

Layout and design by Hybridesign

Printed and bound by Paarl Print

TABLE OF CONTENTS

FOREWORD

Like an unexpected thunderstorm, the 'xenophobic' attacks swept across our country with unprecedented horror and unabated anger. The warning signs were very much in place before the full onslaught happened. But somehow we were completely unprepared as a nation for the unleashing of such violence towards some of the most vulnerable people in our midst. The image of a pleading, burning Mozambican met by laughing onlookers is etched in our memories. Is this what we have come to?

Xenophobic attacks were not unknown in South Africa, but their manifestation in this instance was distinctive in several respects.

Firstly, the attacks were on black foreign nationals. There is no record as far as I understand of any whites or Indians being caught up in the attacks. It does seem as if these categories fall into another classification, i.e. tourist, visitor, investor or something far more elevated.

Secondly, although many nasty things might well have been said to the wealthier of those foreign nationals amongst us, by and large it was the poorer and more vulnerable foreign nationals that were exposed to the most vicious onslaught. As we know, some of those who were most seriously affected had been in the country for more than 35 years and the attacks destabilised their entire livelihood and family.

Thirdly, at least a third of the people killed were South African and so the violence was visited on the particularly marginalised of our society, taking on ethnic and xenophobic connotations. There were 62 people killed in the attacks; tens of thousands of people were displaced and fled for their lives to police stations and other places of safety.

Clearly, these attacks have exposed a raw nerve in society. One can see from the deluge of donations and gifts and compassion that this issue deeply affected the nation. It somehow exposed the fact that after 14 years of democracy all is far from well in the psyche of the people. It seems as if the nation is suspicious and fearful and vexed with profound disparities between the haves and the have-nots. Whether that disparity is felt more keenly in discrimination with regard to service delivery or whether it is an indication that we have not transformed as a nation in our political mindset is a moot point. The fact is that we are in a state of great ambiguity and dysfunction.

It would not be completely fair if one also did not note that the entire phenomenon of migration has become more and more of a global issue. More people, for whatever reason, are wanting to explore, to migrate, to seek different opportunities for their lives, and the global community is going to be faced with the issue of how to respond appropriately to this phenomenon. There is no doubt that the way in which we treat the stranger reflects our humanity; whether that stranger be from another country or whether those strangers be strange because they are poor is beside the point. If we are going to survive as a human race we are going to have to reassess our fundamental value system.

How do we begin to estimate the value of the vast array of skills and giftedness of those who visit our shores, albeit for five to ten years? How do we begin to enable them to make the kind of contribution to this nation that is transformative and enables us to become more part of the world community and, more specifically, part of the African continent? What kind of curricula should be introduced into our educational institutions to ensure that people are not only computer literate, but are skilled in human relationships and able to deal with their prejudices and fears? How finally do we address our economic philosophies to ensure that poverty is an historical fact by the year 2015?

The contributors to this volume, and the colloquium at Wits University upon which it is based, do not address these large and daunting questions directly. But together, the authors demonstrate why it is so crucial that we face them squarely and unflinchingly if we are to create the kind of human community that we wish to be.

Bishop Paul Verryn

INTRODUCTION

FACING THE OTHER AT THE GATES OF DEMOCRACY

ERIC WORBY, SHIREEN HASSIM AND TAWANA KUPE

On the evening of Sunday, 11 May 2008, a gang of young men in Johannesburg's Alexandra township forced their way into a hostel on London Road and initiated a merciless attack on residents they deemed to be 'foreigners'. From this spark, the murder, rape, and looting directed at the bodies and belongings of non-South Africans had spread within days from Alex to informal settlements in Diepsloot and the East Rand, where a Mozambican man, Ernesto Alfabeto Nhamuavhe, was burned alive while bystanders laughed. Soon thereafter, similar attacks began to unfold in the provinces of KwaZulu-Natal and the Eastern and Western Cape. South African citizens speaking the 'wrong' languages – XiTsonga or SiPedi, for example – were also subjected to violent assault. By the time the violence subsided in early June, some 62 people had died – a third of them South

African. Hundreds had suffered grievous injuries and tens of thousands had been displaced from their homes, taking shelter in community halls and police stations, or fleeing in terror across the borders in anticipation of an uncertain future.

AN ANXIOUS RESPONSE

Every instance of large-scale civilian violence towards the innocent provokes a response from those not immediately touched by it. Yet in the catalogue of human brutality unfolding daily around the world, 62 murders over a period of three weeks seems barely worth notice. How many times, over the past five years, have roughly that number of bodies been torn apart by a single bomb in a crowded market in Basra or Baghdad? In a blood-soaked, mediatised world, everyday ethnic or religious violence – much less organised warfare – evokes little more than indifference from the jaded audiences of CNN and BBC World.

Yet the South African story clearly struck a nerve, arousing moral outrage on a global scale: 'The world watched in shock as a wave of xenophobic violence engulfed South Africa,' wrote a journalist for Spiegel International Online in an article that bore the title 'South Africa disgusted with itself'[1]. Had the dream of democratic redemption and reconciliation embodied in the saintly figure of Nelson Mandela reverted to the nightmare of internecine hatred and warfare? Had the daring declaration in South Africa's pioneering Constitution – *South Africa belongs to all who live in it'* – been dismissed with contempt by the chanting of xenophobic slogans and the flourishing of machetes?

That the events of May 2008 generated profound *national* shock and soul-searching also requires explanation. After all, this was hardly the first expression of post-apartheid violence targeting 'foreigners': Somali traders had been systematically burned out of their shops in the Port Elizabeth township of Motherwell in February 2007, stranding some 400 refugees, while as recently as March 2008, four 'foreigners' had been killed in Mamelodi township in Pretoria.[2] One of the country's largest circulation newspapers, the *Daily Sun*, was happy to feed its readership evidence of a truth they found to be self-evident – that 'aliens' were primarily responsible for unemployment and crime.[3] A national opinion survey conducted in 2007 indicated that over 80 per cent of South Africans felt that the government should 'severely limit immigration into the country from troubled African countries'.[4] Not surprisingly, the Nepad peer-review of South Africa felt the need to highlight that South Africa had failed to adequately protect its immigrant population.[5] The surprise and anxiety triggered by the violence of May derive from the implosion of a fantasy – the fantasy of an inclusive 'rainbow' nation whose citizens regard difference not merely with tolerance, but with respect.

NAMING THE VIOLENCE

The very first news reports out of Alexandra township were quick to attach the label 'xenophobic violence' to both individual acts (whether looting shops and shacks, or beating, shooting and raping people) and to the totality of events. Yet soon enough the question of how the violence should be properly *named* became a site of contention and debate, signalling just how much was at stake in determining how the violence should be properly *explained*. More than anything else, the naming debate opens up the question of responsibility: who is to blame and who should ultimately be held accountable for what occurred?

In a characteristically florid speech that invoked a long genealogy of pan-Africanist black South African intellectuals, President Thabo Mbeki rejected the xenophobia explanation at a memorial gathering for victims of the violence:

When I heard some accuse my people of xenophobia, of hatred of foreigners, I wondered what the accusers knew about my people, which I did not know ...The dark days of May which have brought us here today were visited on our country by people who acted with criminal intent. What happened during these days was not inspired by a perverse nationalism, or extreme chauvinism, resulting in our communities violently expressing the hitherto unknown sentiment of mass and mindless hatred of foreigners – xenophobia ... and this I must also say – none in our society has any right to encourage or incite xenophobia by trying to explain naked criminal activity by cloaking it in the garb of xenophobia.[6]

The term 'xenophobia', so Mbeki implies, had been nothing more than a diverting mask used by the perpetrators themselves to justify their contempt for the law, while dangerously inciting others to do the same. In implying that the perpetrators were not 'my people', but 'criminals' who stand outside the polity, Mbeki suggested that *authentic* South Africans, the heirs to a struggle for African unity and redemption that he traces back to the mid-nineteenth century, could not possibly harbour such xenophobic sentiments and motives. Of course it is no small irony that the category of 'criminals' and that of 'immigrants' – taken *together* – make it possible to imagine the category of the virtuous national citizen in the first place.[7]

Most of the contributors to this book also argue that xenophobia is too easy a label, albeit for rather different reasons to those offered by President Mbeki. As they demonstrate from a multiplicity of perspectives, it is perhaps easy enough to make xenophobia – stigmatised as an irrational, bigoted, and personal sentiment – into an alibi for a much more profound social and political malaise. Xenophobia, after all, is often thought by elites to be a deficiency of character and education, a 'popular' disposition to which civilised, cosmopolitan people are relatively immune.[8]

But once xenophobia is accepted to be a secondary symptom rather than a primary cause of violence, responsibility and accountability must necessarily be more widely distributed. To say that the motives of the perpetrators and the precipitating causes of their actions can be explained in terms other than their own stated resentment of foreigners – whether by conditions of acute deprivation, or perceptions of injustice, or a crisis of unfulfilled expectations, or incitement by an incendiary cocktail of popular media, police brutality and political opportunism – is to raise the uncomfortable prospect that their feelings, if not their actions, may be justified. Responsibility, in this view, extends to the business and political classes, and perhaps especially to the middle class South Africans among them who watched the violence unfold on the evening television news in the comfort of suburban sitting rooms, while their gardens were being pruned by undocumented Zimbabweans, Mozambicans and Malawians.

THE ILLUSION OF INCLUSION

Whether cynically or sincerely, the perpetrators of the violence in May explicitly targeted *amakwerekwere* – people who were

6

THIS CHEERY, MULTICOLOURED METAPHOR SEEMS AT BEST SHALLOW AND INCOMPLETE, AT WORST HOLLOW AND INSINCERE.

identified as not properly belonging to the South African nation. But where did such an idea and its justification come from? Wasn't the most fundamental ethic underpinning the transition from authoritarianism to democratic governance one of *inclusion* – not merely the demand to tolerate difference but to actively celebrate it? Isn't that what the globally admired 'rainbow nation' was intended to signify? In the wake of the violence, this cheery, multicoloured metaphor seems at best shallow and incomplete, at worst hollow and insincere.

The violence that seeks to dispossess those identified as 'Other' to the nation is revelatory of the unfinished and contradictory nature of the transition from the authoritarian apartheid project. A decade and a half after the transition to democracy, vast numbers of South Africans feel anything but included in the nation's rainbow. Despite considerable effort, the post-apartheid state has been unable to provide even basic entitlements of safety, health and the right to secure the means of life. In the absence of this kind of fundamental protection, people are abandoned by the state and thrown back onto their own resources for survival. To live in a shack, without any prospect of regular employment, to be destined to die a slow and undignified death from AIDS or tuberculosis, is to live in a condition of abjection – to be consigned to bare life beyond the limits of the political community. In the new South Africa as in the old, killing and being killed are normalised because people are always dying anyway.[9]

Perhaps Archbishop Desmond Tutu's critics were right, and the ethic of tolerant cohabitation implied by the 'rainbow nation' metaphor was never anything more than a useful fiction for

South African elites. As Cathi Albertyn points out in her chapter, the assertion that 'South Africa belongs to all who live in it, black and white' expressed an aspiration for those who formulated the Freedom Charter in 1955. For the framers of the post-apartheid Constitution, the same phrase was intended to take 'us' further down the road on that long walk to freedom. But precisely who was to be among us remains unclear in the slippage between the Constitution's emphasis on residence and popular perceptions of authentic *citizens*.

The aspiration to democratic inclusion also remains haunted by the older, naturalised differences engendered by apartheid ideology. The liberal nationalist model proffered by the African National Congress (ANC) was an explicit response to ethnic nationalism, projecting an inclusive citizenship against the supposedly narrower 'tribal' vision of Mangosuthu Buthelezi and the other homeland leaders. The ANC's 'modern' vision of a post-apartheid democratic citizen, stripped of ethnic or racial differences, aspired to eliminate the expression of identity-based opposition, whether such opposition was grounded in the fears of minorities such as Indians and whites, or smaller, African ethno-linguistic groupings. At the same time, however, strategies to deracialise economic power and to redress economic inequality, such as black economic empowerment and affirmative action, have reinscribed difference as the basis of entitlement.

Difference and entitlement are coupled in new ways around gender as well as race. As Pumla Gqola argues in her chapter, negrophobic xenophobia is 'couched as a battle between two sets of men'. The entitlement claims of 'authentic' male citizens are staked through claims made on 'our' women. The anxieties

SOUTH AFRICA BELONGS TO ALL WHO LIVE IN IT, BLACK AND WHITE.

provoked by economic exclusion and social fragmentation have found expression in violent masculinities, in which weapons are an extension of maleness, and women are no more than bodies to be possessed. Paradoxically, at precisely the moment in which women are claiming rights and asserting their collective presence as political and moral agents, they are being beaten back by the blatant assertion of male power. In a kind of perverse inversion of women's struggle to make gender identity a legitimate component in the repertoire of political action, it was *masculinity* that was performed in the attacks on foreigners.

If the idea of a 'nonracial' virtuous citizen does not entirely succeed in silencing the articulation of *any* identity claim, it nevertheless establishes normative rules about *how* identity can be claimed and in what contexts such claims are permissible, lest one be branded as a political reactionary. To enter the democratic political arena you have to abide by the rules governing the use of identity terms: the recognition of race, class and ethnic identities – especially insofar as they mark structured inequalities – are to be left at the door. Part of the shock of the attacks was the political incorrectness of the language in which they were justified and explained by perpetrators and sympathisers. But the rhetoric of a nonracial democracy cannot ultimately disguise the limits of promising political inclusion as the only route through which to resolve difference.

As the contributions to this volume by Stephen Gelb and Devan Pillay both suggest, political equality is an inadequate answer to the deep social and economic inequalities that apartheid bequeathed. It is difficult to overlook the irony that a black-led state has, through its own deliberate policy choices, continued to demean and debase the daily lives of the very black

XENOPHOBIA

WHO IS TO BLAME
AND WHO SHOULD ULTIMATELY
BE HELD ACCOUNTABLE FOR
WHAT OCCURRED?

citizens it claims to represent. It would hardly be the first time, but dispossessed black South Africans had the right to expect something more than the pleasure of seeing some of their own in the Union Buildings and others driving luxury cars. That the poor have made scapegoats of foreign blacks is a reflection of the political impasse on the long walk to freedom.

There can be little question, after May 2008, that the supposedly slain beast of ethnic nationalism has been resurrected in the fertile terrain of poverty and inequality. The script that is handed to the poor, the marginalised, the excluded, asks them to accept passive representation – certainly not to express atavistic longings or the violent claiming of authenticity, as Daryl Glaser points out. Mbeki's fantasy of an African Renaissance, in which 'his people' would imagine themselves as Africans first, and South Africans second, rings hollow for most of his citizens.

THE RAINBOW BECOMES AN ONION

There are at least three alternative ways of modelling political inclusion in the democratic nation-state. The most conservative is an extension of the nineteenth-century European romantic ideal, with its emphasis on nation as common blood and belonging based on an ideal of ethno-linguistic homogeneity. At the other extreme lies the model that prioritises common democratic values – a citizenship that is chosen and made rather than given and claimed. In between lies the model chosen by the ANC and embodied in the Constitution – a democratic, civic republicanism that nevertheless holds onto the idea of nation as the anchor of citizenship. The 'rainbow nation' rather dissolved than celebrated difference.

Now, in the view of many South Africans, it seems that the rainbow has been displaced by the onion: a way of imagining degrees of national belonging, layered around an authentic core. In this view, the fragile outer skin is made up of black African immigrants: Somalians, Congolese, Zimbabweans. Beneath that fragile exterior – so easily exfoliated and discarded – lie the Tsonga, Shangaan, Venda and Pedi, people with a firmer claim to inclusion, but on the periphery of the political heartland and therefore of dubious loyalty to the national project. In the vortex of the attacks, those testing for authenticity and looking for deserving victims used the Old Testament technique of the shibboleth, demanding of those whose true nationality remained in doubt to correctly render the IsiZulu word for elbow – *indololwane* – or face the brutal consequences.[10]

Yet this ethno-nationalist diagnostic was only applied to blacks – as though centuries of race-based violence by whites were no longer worthy of memory. White foreigners were safe from attacks, insulated in the wealthy neighbourhoods of the city. A number of commentators, including Pumla Gqola and Andile Mngxitama in this volume, have given the name 'negrophobia' to this coupling of historical amnesia with displaced anger and black self-loathing. Darker skin betrays foreign African origins and invites persecution by fellow 'blacks' who see their lighter skin as the most telling signifier of South African belonging. This agonising misrecognition of the 'true' enemy – whether it be expressed in terms of race (through the old apartheid idiom of 'black on black violence') or in terms of class (what some have sardonically referred to as 'shack on shack violence') – suggests a failure of radical as well as liberal politics in the post-

YET THIS ETHNO-NATIONALIST DIAGNOSTIC WAS ONLY APPLIED TO BLACKS – AS THOUGH CENTURIES OF RACE-BASED VIOLENCE BY WHITES WERE NO LONGER WORTHY OF MEMORY.

16

apartheid era. Commentators on the left have been reluctant to acknowledge the ease with which even the most organised and ideologically sophisticated forms of grassroots protest have taken a nationalist, 'xenophobic' turn. Two months before the attacks began in Alexandra, for example, local women in the Anti-Privatisation Forum launched a protest demanding the eviction of a*makwerekwere* who, they argued, had bribed their way into accessing government housing.[11]

These expressions of injury and resentment appear perverse in relation to the political logic of enlightened struggle and the comfortable conceits of politically correct speech. In this respect, the extent to which violence ostensibly aimed at *outsiders* would re-ignite a debate about South Africa's social and political *interior* – and specifically about the shifting articulation of race and class – is striking. The effect has been both to enable and to incite people to talk about things that have been suppressed or forbidden in post-apartheid discourse.

Much of that talk offends the liberal ear, resuscitating racial essentialisms that were the stock in trade of apartheid rule; but in a context where race classification continues to be used as an instrument of post-apartheid restitution, it would be naïve to expect that race-based identities would be consigned to the dustbin of lived social history. To take just one exemplary instance, in the immediate wake of the May violence, a case challenging how the state should classify South Africans of Chinese origin who were citizens before 1994 came before the Pretoria High Court. The judges ruled that for purposes of black economic empowerment legislation, such people were legitimately entitled to identify themselves as 'coloured' – itself an identity label that has been deeply contested by those who claim it as well as by those to whom it has been applied.[12]

The Minister of Labour's response to the ruling laid bare the way in which *racial* othering could be brought into alignment with the othering of the *foreigner*. 'What I know is that coloureds don't speak Chinese,' he said, after suggesting that members of the South African Chinese community habitually pretended not to understand English or Afrikaans when their shops and factories were raided for labour law violations: 'They can speak Chinese, of course, in their homes; I have absolutely no difficulty with that; but when we visit them [i.e. inspect their factories], they must also remember that they are now coloureds … one would not expect a coloured person to ill-treat other coloureds, or black people to ill-treat blacks.'[13]

An outsider might not hear the intended sarcasm of the minister's remarks. But it was not missed by members of the South African Chinese community who were at pains, in their response, to distinguish themselves from *foreign* newcomers from China. Unlike many of those recent immigrants, *we* suffered from the discriminatory exclusions of the Group Areas Act. As a result, few of us own factories and, in case you didn't notice, we've been speaking English and Afrikaans for generations.

These debates around race, law and national belonging are hardly benign. The fear that there are foreign dissimulators and traitors in our midst – Chinese who are cynically and instrumentally claiming to be coloured, Mozambicans who claim to be South African Shangaans – is an all-too-familiar part of the genocide repertoire. The operative logic here is that the truth of the traitor's identity can only be diagnosed through a close examination of skin colour and physiognomy, through the test of linguistic facility (the shibboleth) or worse: through rape, torture and vivisection.[14]

THE LIMITS OF THE STATE

The violence of May drew forth reactions of horror and shame from liberals, communists, and ANC nationalists alike – how could one *not* express these sentiments and still lay claim to a modern, democratic political purpose? Violence beyond that which is authorised by the state defines the limit of political value: it must be disciplined and punished. But the eruption of civilian violence placed the capacity of the state to contain and control under scrutiny. So was its capacity to secure for citizens the right to a decent life, notably through the provision of jobs and housing. As Melinda Silverman and Tanya Zack observe in their contribution here, the post-apartheid regime has, in fact, done reasonably well in providing housing stock for the poor in terms of a modernist planning ethos. But the forms in which housing has been built and provided, and the rules through which housing access has been allocated, bear only a tenuous relation to the far messier reality that shapes the lives of the poor.

In fact, as Noor Nieftagodien's historically-informed analysis of Alexandra township suggests, the very success of the Alexandra Renewal Project's effort to provide housing has reinforced long-standing distinctions between entitled insiders and illegitimate outsiders, who are perceived to be trying to jump the queue. By naming foreigners as ineligible for state housing, the government contracts the constitutional aspirations to include 'all who live here' to a narrow emphasis on 'citizens'.

THE SUPPOSEDLY SLAIN BEAST OF ETHNIC NATIONALISM HAS BEEN RESURRECTED IN THE FERTILE TERRAIN OF POVERTY AND INEQUALITY.

The process of 'service delivery', then, is not merely a question of whether or not the state is capable of meeting the needs of poor people; in its policies and rules of access, it constitutes the authentic citizen.

The modern nation-state form is territorial. Unambiguously bounded, its borders ideally serve as membranes where the ingress and egress of people and things can be monitored, filtered and policed. As David Coplan observes in his contribution here, this theory of the border in South Africa bears only a distant resemblance to the real economy in which civil servants, border police, informal brokers and would-be immigrants negotiate the terms of human movement. The actual provisions of the law remain unknown to most of the participants, although 'the Law' may be bluntly invoked in order to gain leverage or to justify coercion. For some, this is an instance of the profound failure of the state to realise its responsibilities to citizens, who are unjustly left to fight for limited resources with those who are not legally entitled to benefit from them. For others, it suggests a more radical demand for the abolition of borders altogether.[15]

Police everywhere make their living by exercising discretion along the border that separates the legal from the illegal, and the ethical community from 'criminals'. In South Africa, the capacity to use that discretion provides a steady flow of supplementary income in the form of bribes extorted from migrants. As Julia Hornberger points out in her essay here, the recent investment in community policing as a strategy to legitimise state authority has reinforced the scapegoating of migrants as outsiders and criminals. When the attacks began, and victims took refuge in police stations, the police were caught in a genuine dilemma: would their defense and protection of migrants be construed as a betrayal of the authentic community? What would it mean for police to arrest perpetrators for attacking the very 'foreigners' whom the police had previously helped to stigmatise as criminals?

THE NATION RE-IMAGINED

For better or worse, the violence of May 2008 has enabled a forbidden public conversation about race, class and citizenship to spring up through the cracks emerging in the liberal nationalist project. As the violence spread from Alex to Diepsloot to the East Rand and the Central Business District of Johannesburg, the middle class left found itself back on the streets, marching through Hillbrow alongside the poor. The academics and senior leadership of the University of the Witwatersrand and the University of Johannesburg were incited not only to speak but to take to the streets. [16]

The vacuum in the political imagination and practice of the government is rapidly being filled by new visions of society – some darkly bidding for an ever more narrow and exclusionary nationalism, others beckoning towards a more equitable, inclusive and cosmopolitan political order. There can be no doubt that the violence of May 2008 marked more than a terrible and terrifying turning point in the lives of tens of thousands of poor people living in South Africa. It marked a turning point in the conversation about this country's self-representation as a political community and about the specific meaning of race and nation, as well as class and citizenship. It remains to be seen where that conversation will lead and what difference it will make to the lives of all who live in South Africa.

On 28 May 2008, two and a half weeks after the attacks began to be unleashed against 'foreigners' and those who sought to defend them in Alexandra township, the Faculty of Humanities in the University of the Witwatersrand convened an urgent colloquium on Violence and Xenophobia in South Africa: Critical Responses. *It was attended by approximately 250 people from Wits and the wider Johannesburg community, who stayed for nearly five hours of intense, often emotional reflection and debate. Nearly 20 people – mostly Wits academics from a variety of disciplines, but also two student leaders, a journalist and a bishop – were asked to make formal presentations. Their brief was to address the unfolding violence in ways that were conversant with the moment, yet rooted in scholarship and ongoing research. The colloquium aimed to draw upon that deep scholarship and expertise to engage in the search for short and long term solutions that would promote an ethos of peace, inclusiveness, humanity and security.*

This volume, which emanates directly from the colloquium, is intended to offer critical analysis that helps to make sense of the nuances and trajectories of building a democratic society out of a deeply divided and conflictual past, and in the conditions of global recession, heightening inequalities, and future uncertainty.

We are grateful to all of the presenters and colleagues at Wits for their contribution to making the colloquium into such a moving and effective vehicle for the development of collective insight into profoundly unsettling events. We are appreciative of the exceptional effort made by all of our contributors to generate texts of high quality and relevance under ridiculously tight deadlines.

Iriann Haupt and Tara Polzer responded to our request for help with great generosity.

We thank Alon Skuy for his courageous, powerful and evocative images that document the events analysed here. And above all, we are deeply indebted to the extraordinary commitment of Veronica Klipp and the rest of the editorial and design team at Wits University Press, as well as Barbara Ludman and Karen Lilje, who combined their talent and energy to generate a volume of such high quality in such a remarkably compressed time frame. We acknowledge, with gratitude, the generosity of the Ford Foundation for their financial contribution towards the production of this book.

A TORN NARRATIVE OF VIOLENCE

BY ALEX ELISEEV

Moments from the xenophobic mayhem flash in my memory like a strobe light. Perhaps the torn narrative is the result of coming too close to the bloodshed. Or maybe it's just the way I've remembered it, working to meet deadlines for a newspaper that changes its front page four times a day.

As a reporter for *The Star*, I was dispatched to cover the violence on the afternoon of 12 May – a day after the mayhem began on the dark streets of Alexandra. In one night, more than 60 people had been attacked. I remember arriving at London Road and seeing hundreds of people fleeing the township, their belongings piled up on the pavements as they raced to beat the sunset. Many had no idea where they were going. One woman – a foreigner – had spent the night hiding under her bed as her husband stood guard at the door. She had lived in Alexandra, in peace, for five years.

Suddenly, up the road, a gang ran up behind a youth and flung a brick at his head. He collapsed on the ground, his head falling at the edge of the pavement. Blood flowed down into the gutter and was carried off by a small stream .

That night we filed our stories inside the police's heavily-armoured Nyala as it drove up and down the township, police officers firing rubber bullets into the alleys.

The storm was just beginning, but from our position at the epicentre it was clear that something was very wrong. 'Outside the bulletproof glass [of the Nyala] something frightening has engulfed Alexandra,' I wrote at the time. 'The scenes that play out in the streets belong somewhere else. Anywhere but in the new South Africa.'

Technology allows experts to forecast deadly storms and raise the alarm. But in this case, the service delivery protests and scattered murders of foreigners near Pretoria and in the Western Cape were almost entirely under the radar. And then, after one night of bloodlust, the storm struck.

For most of the first week we covered Alexandra. We watched as bodies turned up in the dusty slivers between shacks. As mobs went on the rampage in Extension 7, forcing residents to show them their identity books, I remember a vicious stick fight that began in slow motion and then turned into a bloody blur. Police sprayed tear gas into the faces of the men and shoved them into police vans – but the violence was swelling.

We piled into Toyota Tazzes and tore around the township in packs made up of crews from various newspapers, radio and television stations. We took cover inside Metro Police vans as the rocks rained down, shaking the vehicles as they found their target.

AND THEN, AFTER ONE NIGHT OF BLOODLUST, THE STORM STRUCK.

THERE WAS NO COUNT OF HOW MANY PEOPLE HAD BEEN KILLED, WOUNDED, RAPED OR DISPLACED.

AND THERE WAS SILENCE FROM OUR LEADERS.

We ran with the panga-wielding mobs and then behind the police officers with their shotguns. We took frantic calls from our editors who tried to pull us out of the danger zones.

We wrote our notes as police saturated the area, battling the mobs, while their stations filled up with thousands of refugees. The foreigners – many in the country illegally – were so desperate they were turning to their enemy for protection.

By Thursday, the violence had been quelled. There was no count of how many people had been killed, wounded, raped or displaced. And there was silence from our leaders.

A week of savagery wound down and for two or three days there was little bloodshed. The skies were clear of the black smoke that had been rising from the flames cleansing communities of unwanted residents. It felt as if the worst was behind us.

That Saturday I spent in the Pilanesberg nature reserve. The contrast of what I had witnessed during the week, and what surrounded me in the sanctuary, was surreal.

I left early on Sunday morning and by early afternoon I was in a squatter camp in Honeydew, moving on later to Diepsloot. The violence had spread like wildfire across the province and my colleagues were dispatched across Ekurhuleni.

Exactly a week after the first attacks, the real nightmare had become visible. The eye of the storm had passed, and what came now found its way on to the front pages of newspapers across the globe.

As Ernesto Nhamuave, a miner from Mozambique, was stabbed, beaten and set on fire, the course of South Africa's history shifted. That moment – with its angry orange flames and dark plumes of smoke – allowed the press to drag the horror inside the rainbow

I LOOKED DOWN AND SAW RED.

nation's townships into the living rooms of the wealthy, into the hallways of the Union Buildings and across the borders.

The following nights, in Diepsloot, the danger of what we were doing set in. We were wearing bulletproof jackets and trailing police across the pitch-black settlement. I remember a bullet passing over our heads and the sound it made as it sliced through the air. I recall how we ducked behind a giant waste bin as rubber rounds bounced off the shacks around us like the inside of an old pinball machine.

Tuesday morning brought more horror. Before sunrise we were in Ramaphosa, watching the sky for smoke and listening to the radio. Luckily Shayne Robinson – the photographer I was working with – had brought a flask of hot coffee. I stood next to Joao Silva, one of the legendary Bang Bang Club photographers who had documented the country's turbulent townships in the early 1990s. I never imagined I would work alongside Silva in the burning settlements. 'It's déjà vu,' he said.

That morning we went to the scene of three small houses that had been petrol bombed. We were first to discover the flames and called the firefighters. Small suitcases had been neatly packed but abandoned in the yard.

From there we sped to a mine hostel in Reiger Park. There was word that several miners had been attacked during the night. Shayne pulled our Opel Corsa into the yard and brought it to a stop on the gravel. We jumped out and I walked towards the police's Nyala. As I arrived at its back tyre, I realised I had stepped in a deep puddle. I looked down and saw red.

From there the blood trails ran around a corner and into a dry mielie patch. They led us to three bodies, lying face down in thick

blood. Their heads were swollen and the skin had broken from the beating. Like bags of trash, they had been dragged out of the hostel and dumped in the back.

When I looked at the scene all I could see were the images that emerged from Rwanda. Later, our newspaper ran the photograph of the hostel massacre next to a file photograph of Rwanda's genocide and the similarity was as frightening as it was in my mind. Miraculously, two of the men were still fighting for their lives. They were taken to hospital, but it is not known whether they survived.

At the hostel, an old man with a deep wound through his eyebrow told us that a mob had arrived the previous night and had gone room-to-room hunting foreigners.

They had beaten one to death and left him in room 21. Three had been dragged outside and he had escaped to tell the tale. But when I returned to the hostel later, in search of the names of the slain, it emerged that the mob had vented their fury on the old and the weak. The man murdered in room 21 was 76 years old and a South African citizen. The one attacked in room 51 was nearly 60. The man who survived, and told the media how the attackers had used steel pipes to beat their victims, was also 76. Like predators in the wild, the mob had gone for easy targets.

For me, the hostel massacre defined the xenophobic attacks. The mob arrived under cover of night and began searching the hostel – knowing that foreigners from Mozambique come to South Africa to take jobs on the mines. They were a fearless, faceless mob accusing their victims of taking their jobs. They went from door to door and sniffed out the foreigners. They tortured them and dragged them – feet first – out of the hostel, sending their

THE MAN MURDERED IN ROOM 21 WAS 76 YEARS OLD AND A SOUTH AFRICAN CITIZEN.

message of hate. The victims lay in the field all night as police failed to arrive. And in the wake of the attack, hundreds of miners fled in fear. A secret safe house was eventually set up for them by the mine.

In Ramaphosa, we continued to cover the violence. We ran with the mobs as they chased foreigners up the mine dumps, scraping their machetes against the ground.

We found another man who had been beaten and set on fire. The locals told us he was dead and called us to have a look. When we got there it turned out he was alive but paralyzed by pain, his legs soaked in blood. We called for help and police carried him out of the township on a mattress.

Some of the time we waited on the outskirts, watching as victims were brought out. Panic in their eyes. Blood drying on their skin. Steel cords wrapped around their throats.

We also worked inside the township, where tense negotiations were shattered with a single glass bottle crashing at the feet of the Metro Police, where a photographer was shot with live buckshot and a victim of rubber bullets lay semi-conscious with an axe tucked into his underwear.

During that week cars burned, helicopters swooped to the ground to disperse crowds and the army was eventually called in. The number of refugees grew into tens of thousands and by the end of the week the violence had spread as far as Cape Town.

I remember working until three in the morning, filing stories by four and going home to crash, then waking up and doing it all over again. We were running on adrenalin. And it was incredible how quickly it drained out of your body once an assignment was finished.

THE STORM HAD PASSED.
BUT ITS BLOODY WINDS HAVE CHANGED US FOREVER.

The politicians were doing damage control as the death toll climbed towards 60. The weeks that followed exposed the true size of the refugee crisis, and brought with it the humanitarian disasters. The focus shifted, and South Africans opened their hearts to support those caught up in the violence. Protests against the attacks were organised and the country began dealing with the aftermath while trying to understand what could have caused such an abomination. The long process of re-integration, or escape, began. Life began to tick over again.

The storm had passed. But its bloody winds have changed us forever.

I DID NOT EXPECT SUCH A THING TO HAPPEN

ROLF MARUPING[1]

My parents came from Mozambique but I was born here in South Africa. I have spent my entire life here and all my friends are from here. I lost my mother in June 2004 and my father in October the same year. They left me a stand in Makawuso and I was sustaining myself from the money tenants paid. I was too young to look for employment then but at least with the shacks I could survive. I tried to send myself to school for about one year but then I dropped out. I love music and singing hip-hop. I am looking forward to getting a sponsor so that I may create my own band and succeed in my dream.

I met this white guy who was into assisting disadvantaged kids and he hired my friend and me to assist him. I had hoped that the little money that I used to get from this white guy's project would at least give me an opportunity to upgrade my studies, but because he abandoned it due to the attacks I am now doomed.

When all this violence took place I was at work, where I repair radios and TVs. I knocked off around 8 pm. When I got home my aunt asked me to go to her place to check the situation as she had been chased away in the afternoon. I found that they had not yet broken down the gate and doors and it was still secured.

I returned to my place and found it in a chaotic state, as people were being attacked and trying to flee. It was dark. While I stood with friends outside my house, a group of about 12 youths came armed with knives, iron bars, hammers, spears and all sorts of weapons. They said, 'We want this guy who fixes radios and TVs' and they meant myself. I said, 'I don't know this guy you are talking about.' They found my shack locked and went their way. But then this other woman they met advised them that the person they were looking for was the one they had just left alone.

That's when I jumped the fence and fled and joined the other people running away. We spent Sunday at the police station. On Monday I decided to go back to check my place and I was astonished to find it razed down. There was nothing remaining. They looted all my belongings and then removed the zinc sheets. There had been four shacks and they had looted all of them.

The attackers even attacked the shop of this Indian who was selling affordable goods and one wonders at the logic behind that. It's an Indian, for goodness sake, and not an African, so why bother him? We may have issues as Africans but I see no reason why we should include the Indians.

These guys who were the attackers moved as a group. There were nine people who came in the afternoon and had a meeting with the local committee. When people first saw these young

I JUMPED THE FENCE AND FLED AND JOINED
THE OTHER PEOPLE RUNNING AWAY.

people they thought that it was just some people who had taken too much alcohol and were happy, as they were singing *'Umshini wam'*. But then they led the attacks. These people had regalia that they tied around their heads as a mark of identification. Without it you would be attacked. If you heard them shouting 'Hey comrade' you had to return the greeting by the same *'Hola comrade'* and if you failed you would get attacked. They attacked you so that they could remove your shack and accommodate their relatives.

The local committees never tried to assist us, to reduce the impacts of the violence. Anyway, the committees are not our own making. They just woke up being there. What kind of committee exists without being elected into that office? Before this violence the committee members would patrol the neighborhood at night. They would intercept you if you were travelling at night and they would search you. If you were unlucky, you could lose the cash you were carrying. They would also apprehend robbers. If they confiscated the gun of a robber they would use it instead of handing it to the police. Imagine the amount of money they would make in the one or two years while in office.

I think the committees do not want us to return there. This is because there has been some reallocation of our stands and our goods and they know pretty well that when we return they will not get any financial gains.

Before this violence, my friend Xolani and I worked with this white guy who had computers. At times he would drive us into the shacks. It appears that some people got jealous of this relationship and our progress and they shot my friend and he died. He had bought a flat in Germiston for keeping orphans so that they could get schooling. But the people in the shacks do not want to see someone succeeding. Jealousy is a bad illness for shack dwellers. Instead of admiring what someone has done they would rather kill you for it. All of us get chances from God and at every point in our lives He has plans for us. I had a computer and sound mixers, and so these guys saw fit to disturb my progress by looting my assets and sending me off the settlement.

Not everyone is like that. There was this boy who was coming home in the afternoon during the violence and he met a group of Zulu youths who were on standby, waiting to pounce on such people. When they attacked him, a lady who is also Zulu lay on top of the victim and said, 'It will be better if you kill me but let this innocent boy go'. So they couldn't continue. They said to him, 'You tell your dad that we don't want to see him here and he must leave'. The lady escorted the boy away and he was so grateful for the lady who saved his life.

After the violence I went to my employer and told him that I was going back home to Mozambique and needed money for one or two expenses. But he was not a good man. I expected this guy to understand my plight but he was not prepared to listen. He paid me wages worth one week and withheld the rest that he owed me. He knew that due to the displacement I could not report him because the police were too occupied to attend to my case.

I did think of going back to Mozambique but I am staying with a lady, a South African, and I could not just let her go like that. She is pregnant. My fiancée was also ejected from the shacks – they told her to follow her Shangaan man. Another man told me that they came to evict his lady from the shacks. They wanted to

JEALOUSY IS A BAD ILLNESS FOR SHACK DWELLERS. INSTEAD OF ADMIRING WHAT SOMEONE HAS DONE THEY WOULD RATHER KILL YOU FOR IT.

hack off the head of their nine-month-old baby. The lady cried until they ordered her to follow her Shangaan boyfriend. It was hard that day. I did not expect such a thing to happen.

During the violence, the police were uncooperative. My aunt phoned them and requested them to assist her with an escort as she had kids. They told her that they could not assist her and then a white guy came to the rescue and left her at the station. She lost a very big home and she has no other home as she had relocated from Mozambique. The neighbours took everything and even used her material to extend their place onto hers. They are even using her pots and pans.

It is hard to believe that it was the people we know who attacked us and not strangers. It would have been better if these people had given us warnings and told us to leave. We would have had time to take our assets with us, not this way of just saying 'Leave now'.

The man who was burnt: what happened is that he went to the police and asked them to assist him after he had been chased from his place by attackers. The police just said, 'Go back, we are behind you and we will find you still on the way.' How can you say that to somebody seeking your help?

The attackers waited for him and when they realised that he was not under police escort they captured him just as he left the station, tied him up, poured paraffin on his body and set him alight. The police did nothing.

This is a small area and the police could have stopped this well before it spread. How could this violence have spread from Pretoria up to this end when we had the police equipped with cars and everything? So it surprises us as to why the attackers

in Makawuso were not caught even up to today. Even right now the police are arresting people and they don't care if you explain that you are from the shelters. They are trying to force people to pay them the little that they have in bribes. It's lucky if you get away without paying but they will punish you by dropping you off far from your place.

The government needs to put in place strong security measures because we cannot go alone to these places. There is still some deep-rooted hatred against the foreigners. People who are tenants at the informal settlement have no problem with accepting us back but those neighbours who looted our assets are the ones who are resisting the move. They know that they can lose our assets back to us. Remember, they have now extended their shacks to our stands and they would be facing the risk of losing that again. There would be fights with the locals as some people may want revenge. You cannot just watch your neighbour utilising what they looted from you.

The only way to deal with this problem is for the government to put up strong legislation that lays down very tough penalties against the perpetrators.

I think the government should hire security personnel drawn from the Zulu, Shangaan, and maybe Zimbabweans. We are nearing the 2010 World Cup, yet foreigners are being evicted, so what signals are we sending to the many foreigners we are expecting in 2010? They will fear coming here and say, 'When we get there they will kill us'. They are well informed through the photos that the media is showing the rest of the world about the violence. Whoever sees those pictures will stay away because they will not want to go to a place where they will be burnt.

I made a decision and said it's better for me to suffer here to see how this may end. I have never been to Mozambique for long because I was born here in South Africa and I don't know anything about home. Where would I start? But here I still have hope that one of these days I will find someone who will be willing to assist me so that I may develop my music talent. Due to my passion in music I even have a plan of recruiting young guys from the shelters here so that I can teach them music and even start a band. But it is difficult. Since my parents are late the entire family is looking up to me for help. There are children who have now dropped out of school because I cannot pay.

I have now forgiven the perpetrators though initially I was very cross with what they did. But I am just thinking of what life we are going to lead now, after we had a good life previously. Even if we can be sent back to the shacks it will be difficult to cohabit again. When I meet a person on the road there won't be any trust because you will now know to which ethnic group you belong.

They should outlaw labelling based on ethnic lines because we are all blacks. You see, with this kind of behaviour they are sending wrong information to the generation of our kids. You now hear someone shouting *'Vimba iShangane'*, catch the Shangaan. You look at the person and discover it's a very small kid. How would you feel?

(DIS)CONNECTIONS

ELITE AND POPULAR 'COMMON SENSE'
ON THE MATTER OF 'FOREIGNERS'

DARYL GLASER

It is striking how great is the disconnect between popular and elite 'common sense' on the matter of 'foreigners'. This xenophobia really is coming up from below – it is profoundly democratic, albeit in the majoritarian-popular sense rather than the liberal-constitutionalist one. The bottom-up character is confirmed by surveys, focus groups and other gauges. It is anyway obvious from, say, watching the huge and sceptical crowd that greeted Zuma during his firefighting trip to the East Rand town of Ekurhuleni or listening, as one cannot avoid doing in this country, to radio talk shows. 'They' – the urban poor – thus occupy a different universe of meaning to 'us' – people who subscribe to internationalist ideologies and enjoy some insulation from daily struggles for material survival.

Xenophobic violence is not coming from the elites – from neither the major parties nor major organised civil society actors, neither the Zuma faction nor the Mbeki one. In fact organisations claiming to be tribunes of the masses, like the Congress of South African Trade Unions, have proven out of touch with the popular pulse on this issue, failing to see recent events coming. (The one partial exception, it seems, is the South African National Civic Organisation, whose xenophobic utterances suggest that it is surprisingly 'grounded' in the poor despite frequently being written off as a ghost formation.)

The country's leaders may bear indirect responsibility through policy failure and acts of commission, but I see no evidence that the marauding crowds are taking their cue from government immigration policy or from corrupt cops who extort bribes from immigrants. We do not have the active anti-xenophobic leadership that we need, but at least there is no Jean-Marie Le Pen or Joerg Haider or Patrick Buchanan mobilising anti-immigrant grievance, at least not at national level. Or – to take examples closer to home (if we can still say that about Africa) – we do not have leading politicians manipulating anti-foreigner sentiment as they have recently done, with calamitous consequences, in the Democratic Republic of the Congo and Ivory Coast. This matters: the absence of elite encouragement may be all that separates what has happened here from what happened in Rwanda.

The truth is that popular democracy in action is not necessarily a pretty sight. We are reminded of why we need a constitutional liberal democracy, even if the latter has its own deficiencies. Vulnerable individuals and minorities need institutional protection from the unmediated expression of popular passions.

THE TRUTH IS THAT POPULAR DEMOCRACY IN ACTION
IS NOT NECESSARILY A PRETTY SIGHT.

(2)

Yet we must avoid, too, any smug attribution of this xenophobic wave to an essential and freestanding evil amongst the poor, or recourse in the assumption that 'they' simply need 'our' moral education. Xenophobia is morally repugnant, of course, but it also has its indirect causes, if by that we mean not ineluctable, choice-denying determinants but patterns of pressure, opportunity, incentive and lived experience that render some ways of seeing and acting more probable than others.

The xenophobic discourse current in South Africa today represents the authentic effort of the subaltern classes to make sense of their condition: nor is their reading irrational. They *are* struggling for scarce urban resources (notably, as Melinda Silverman and Tanya Zack point out in this volume, for housing) and there can be little doubt that immigrants are competing for those resources. The belief that such competition exists is not an instance of false consciousness. Moreover immigrants compete well, because they are less work-fussy, less rights-conscious, more desperate, perhaps sometimes (as certain employers insist) more industrious and skilled. Whereas many comparable developing countries and regions export their poor – Mexico, Central America, the Caribbean, north and west Africa and south Asia – we are importing them in vast numbers, and inviting them to integrate into our societies, without foreign or local assistance. This simply must be causing strain.

(3)

Nor are our elites innocent of generating, indirectly, the kind of climate in which recent violence could flare. Political and

AND THEN OF COURSE THERE IS THE FAILURE OF LEADERSHIP SINCE THE ATTACKS BEGAN.

economic leaders cannot wash their hands of responsibility for policies that have failed to address poverty, unemployment and especially inequality while raising popular expectations. If we have a culture that tolerates crime and violence, a militaristic subculture of 'struggle' originating in the township streets and guerrilla camps of the anti-apartheid period and actively mobilised even now by militants (think of the security guard strike) has contributed to it. Corruption at Home Affairs and other bureaucracies fans popular perceptions that incomers can buy themselves privileged access to resources. Corrupt and incompetent policing, abetted by a government in denial about crime, creates a context in which citizens are tempted by vigilantism, armed by stereotypes about the supposed criminal propensities of particular populations. And then of course there is the failure of leadership since the attacks began.

(4)

While xenophobia helps a part of the masses to render their social landscape intelligible, it simultaneously renders that landscape unintelligible to the elites. Take the race-conscious black middle class that has gathered round President Thabo Mbeki. How are they to shoehorn this xenophobia into their narrative of African solidarity against Western imperialism? *Their* competitors – for professional and business places – are whites. Their white competitors reciprocate this race consciousness. Or the organised labour component of the coalition supporting African National Congress President Jacob Zuma: they compete with capital for the proceeds of production or social surplus, mapping their world in class rather than race terms.

Yet here is the black underclass, mapping human beings along lines of real or perceived nationality – ironically, a sense of nationality that has accreted around territorial boundaries drawn by colonialists. (A testament to the success of post-independence nation-building? Perhaps not: if that project has sought a civic national identity, anti-immigrants appear to attribute ethnic essences to nations. Thus, for example, Shangaan is equated with Mozambican, and tensions between nationalities merge with inter-ethnic ones.)

(5)

Zuma represents a somewhat special case of connection/ disconnection with mass xenophobia.

Quite a few of the violent attackers seem to be from the Zulu working class: associated with hostels, supporting Zuma and singing 'Umshini wam', people who identify with Zuma's folksy ways and anti-establishment streak. In some quarters Zulu-ness seems to have become a standard of South Africanness, with those unversed in Zulu vocabulary liable to be attacked as un-South African.

Yet Zuma, a veteran of exile and African mediation efforts, is comfortable with Africa and the Africans. He cannot be accused of crowd-pleasing populism on this issue, even if he hasn't shown great leadership either. But his connection with a part of the xenophobic constituency does suggest that he has a special duty of leadership here – the sort of special duty he had, and failed to fulfil, when it came to restraining those who gathered outside his 2006 rape trial.

On second thoughts, would Zuma leadership make a difference? Perhaps the Zuma that the masses know and love is a

OF WHAT PROFOUND SOCIAL MALAISE IS

XENOPHOBIA

AND THE VIOLENCE THAT IT INSPIRES

A SYMPTOM?

construct of their imagination; a resilient construct, immune to anything Zuma actually says or does. Still, the duty is there ...

(6)

The fact that the urban poor have made a rational diagnosis of their problem does not mean it is the only possible one, nor that it is morally defensible.

Other possible diagnoses would point, obviously, to (aforementioned) poverty, inequality, unemployment, and to government corruption, incompetence and indifference – not to mention Mbeki's scandalous coddling of Robert Mugabe, the Zimbabwe dictator whose policies have triggered the biggest single wave of refugees fleeing into South Africa. The prescription called for by *this* diagnosis is mobilisation against the powerful in this land, not against the weak. (A national uprising against Mbeki's Zimbabwe policy would be a good start.)

In any event, though, attacking foreigners is morally indefensible, since it violates both duties of justice and humanitarian obligations. By duties of justice I mean duties to refrain from harming others (the most elemental of all) and to give others what we owe them (for example, to fellow Africans in repayment of their sacrifices during the anti-apartheid struggle or their contribution to building our mining industry). By contrast, we have humanitarian obligations to our fellow human beings to make their lives better, irrespective of whether we owe them anything in particular.

It is not self-evident that either of these duties – of justice or humanity – terminate at our borders, or at the borders of the citizen body; if it comes to that, it is not even self-evident, though it is certainly arguable, that we have greater moral duties to compatriots than to humanity as a whole. The best argument against xenophobia is not the precarious one that 'foreigners' benefit our society, but the cosmopolitan one that they are human beings too.

Fulfilling obligations of justice and humanity should not be made to sound easier than it is. It demands sacrifices, and it is unfair to require that the local poor bear a disproportionate share of them. Nor should we be dishonest: unless we have the courage to follow to its logical conclusion a policy of totally open borders, we should acknowledge that some degree of coercive border regulation is unavoidable. But whatever needs to be done to balance our universal duties of justice and humanity with our special obligations to compatriots (including poor compatriots), there can be no place in the correct formula – and there must be zero tolerance – for the kind of violence that has recently bloodied our streets and settlements.

XENOPHOBIA IN ALEXANDRA

NOOR NIEFTAGODIEN

On 11 May 2008 parts of Alexandra, located in the north-eastern suburbs of Johannesburg, exploded into an orgy of xenophobic attacks against foreign Africans. The violence was concentrated in and around the area known as Beirut, the infamous territory around the hostels that witnessed some of the worst civil violence in the early 1990s. During those three or four days in May, two people in Alexandra (including one South African) were killed, at least 60 injured and hundreds were forcibly evicted from their homes by gangs of armed young men. Several women were raped. Two young men who evicted a Shangaan-speaking man painted the following chilling warning on his shack, which they had taken over:

Uzofa uma ngikuthola ngoba sekweyami UKhuzwayo (You will die if I find you in this shack because it now belongs to me, Khuzwayo).[1]

This episode of xenophobic violence involved the poor fighting against the poor, even if only for the right to occupy a dilapidated shack. What brought about such utter desperation, and why in Alexandra?

Xenophobic violence seems completely incongruous with the history of Alexandra. After all, the township has a proud tradition of radical democratic politics dating back to the squatter movements and bus boycotts of the 1940s and the 1950s. Residents of the area struggled for decades against state efforts to remove the township forcibly as part of apartheid's racial restructuring of the urban areas, and won. In the 1980s residents of Alexandra played a leading role in the anti-apartheid movement and, in many respects, defined radical civic politics. It has also been a home to immigrants and migrants for nearly a century.

More recently, the township has been the site of an ambitious urban renewal project aimed at transforming the area through the provision of housing on a mass scale, creating jobs and generating local economic activity. To some extent, therefore, it is understandable that people have expressed surprise at the outbreak of xenophobic violence in Alexandra. But I argue below that there are important reasons to review these assumptions.

As the violence spread from Alexandra to engulf settlements across Gauteng, especially in Ekurhuleni, the authorities sought to blame criminals, a third force and political conspiracies. It is true that criminality is invariably present during political violence, and that criminal elements took advantage of the chaos in Alexandra to loot people's homes. But these were by-products of the mayhem, not the underlying causes. By defining

PEOPLE HAVE EXPRESSED SURPRISE AT THE OUTBREAK OF XENOPHOBIC VIOLENCE IN ALEXANDRA.

the problem in terms of criminality, the state's intervention has emphasised security-driven solutions. Thus the army has been deployed and the National Intelligence Agency woken from its slumber. While perpetrators of violence and looting must be apprehended, this will not eliminate xenophobia. The state's focus on criminality, as Loren Landau points out in this volume, is best understood as an attempt to deflect attention from the real underlying causes of the crisis.

Any attempt to understand this conflict should be located in the politics of failed development and delivery. Alexandra and other townships that experienced xenophobic violence, such as Ramaphosaville in Ekurhuleni, are still the dumping grounds of the marginalised and alienated. Alexandra is hugely overcrowded, with a population of 350 000, 81 per cent of whom are crammed into the 2km² of old Alexandra. The vast majority of residents live in 74 000 informal structures, of which 34 000 are shacks.

Despite its proximity to industrial areas and to Africa's financial centre, Sandton, the township has hardly benefited from the country's economic growth over the past decade. Unemployment remains stubbornly high at 29 per cent, and 71 per cent of employed people work in unskilled or semi-skilled jobs. As a result income levels are low, with at least 20 per cent of households earning less than R1 000 per month.[2] Many Alexandrans, whose living conditions have not altered since the end of apartheid, thus feel excluded and marginalised from the new South Africa.

The poor people of Alexandra daily eke out an existence in the insalubrious warrens of congested squatter camps and dilapidated prison-like hostels. These environs subject people

ANY ATTEMPT TO UNDERSTAND THIS CONFLICT SHOULD BE LOCATED IN THE POLITICS OF FAILED DEVELOPMENT AND DELIVERY.

to the most degrading conditions. A recent survey of Madala hostel found raw sewerage spilled in corridors, parts of the building falling apart and concluded that 'Not even pigs want to live in this place.'[3] It is no surprise then that hatred has spewed from these places. And, as distasteful as it might be, it is also no surprise when national and ethnic identities are mobilised to evict the 'Other' or 'outsiders' in order to gain access to limited resources.

Since 2005 the pace of delivery by the Alexandra Renewal Project has accelerated. In addition to major electrification schemes and improvements in water supplies, the project has been constructing more than 26 000 houses.[4] Although this figure will not meet the existing housing requirements, the progress made by the project has increased expectations of delivery in the township. These heightened expectations have also been accompanied by growing anxieties about who might be excluded from this process – especially as the project nears the end of its lifespan – which, in turn, have tended to exacerbate existing cleavages between insiders and outsiders.

The distinction between insider and outsider has long defined politics in Alexandra, and is located in the origins of the township. It was informed by the apartheid government's influx control policies, especially the allocation of section 10 rights to certain groups of Africans, which in Alexandra became associated with property ownership. This cleavage manifested itself again in the 1980s in the form of *bona fides* (insiders) versus *amagoduka* (newcomers/rural), under circumstances of extreme social distress caused by the massive influx of people from the rural areas. But those divisions were largely subdued

XENOPHOBIA IS NOT NEW.

at the time by the presence of a mass civic movement and organs of people's power, which created a strong sense of community in the township.

Now insiders are perceived as having a relatively privileged status in the township and most likely to benefit from development. To some extent the dominant discourse and practices of leaders in Alexandra have contributed to the idea that exclusion of outsiders, through removals, is an appropriate means of effecting development. At the genesis of the Alexandra Renewal Project, approximately 3 500 families were forcibly relocated to places far away from Alexandra.[5] Those defined as outsiders, and thus unlikely to benefit immediately from development, struggle to gain access to services. When they make their claims on already scarce resources, they are regarded as a threat to the interests of insiders. Understood in these terms, African foreigners are defined as the quintessential outsider and as the immediate threat to the insiders. Consequently, they are subject to exclusion, even violently so. An unnamed resident expressed his feelings to a local newspaper thus,

> We are fed up with these foreigners. These people come here and take our jobs and accept below inflation salaries. We cannot compete with them because we have families, while they only have themselves to look after.[6]

Such blatantly xenophobic views have been described as being totally incongruous with the new South Africa, and particularly a township like Alexandra. It is true that throughout its history Alexandra has been a place of migrants and immigrants, many

IT IS NO SURPRISE THEN THAT HATRED HAS SPEWED FROM THESE PLACES.

of whom became integrated into the township. But there have also always lurked beneath the surface of communalism varying degrees of antipathy to outsiders. In fact, the post-1994 period has witnessed several instances of xenophobia in the township.

Ironically, the first recorded incident of xenophobia occurred a few months after the 1994 elections. In January 1995 the Alexandra Land and Property Owners Association organised a march of about 400 residents to the police station to demand the 'immediate eviction of foreign residents'. In May 1997 the *Sunday Independent* reported that residents of Maputo section in Setswetla squatter camp, located on the north-eastern border of old Alexandra, and consisting of several Mozambican families, were routinely attacked by groups of youth from the township. Then, as is the case now, police claimed the attacks were part of a general increase in crime in Alexandra.

Xenophobia even reared its head in local progressive movements. During the 2000 occupation of flats on the East Bank, the Alexandra Homeless Youth and Families (AHYF) emerged as a radical voice against efforts by the authorities to prevent local people from gaining access to housing. At the time it led a successful occupation of the flats. During the course of this struggle the AHYF began to direct their anger against African foreigners and vowed not to allow them in their houses. It claimed to 'have information that one Nigerian bought 10 houses', and warned, '[the Nigerians] will not be able to stay in those houses unless they have police guards, day and night'.[7] The AHYF also claimed Alexandra was becoming a 'small Nigeria'.

It is important to acknowledge these earlier episodes of overt xenophobia because they highlight the prevalence of such sentiments. Each incident also revealed a more widespread anti-foreigner sentiment among various layers of the township's population. Xenophobia is not new.

One of the main questions asked about the recent xenophobic violence is who was behind it. In fact, it has proven rather difficult to apportion blame to any one organisation, individual or group. What is clear is that the initial attacks emanated from the hostel and the surrounding shack areas. As a result, Zulu migrants were blamed for the attacks, a view that acquired some credibility when non-Zulu speaking South Africans as well as foreign migrants were attacked. However, other community members also joined in the attacks when the violence spread to other parts of the township, albeit briefly. Young men were the main perpetrators of the violence, although a handful of women participated in the looting and occupation of shacks.

There were three meetings held during the week before the outbreak where it is alleged residents complained about crime in the area, which they blamed on African foreigners. Either during these meetings or immediately afterwards, some residents called for action to be taken against foreigners.

It remains unclear whether any single organisation was behind the violence. Initially accusations were directed at the Alexandra Residents Association, an Inkatha Freedom Party-linked civic organisation led by the Archbishop David Khumalo, who is also the head of the UBuhle Bama Free Apostolic Church in Zion. However, the IFP denied any involvement and its local leader, Nhlanhla Msimang, says he was not only surprised by the attacks, but as soon as he heard hostel dwellers were involved made every effort to bring the situation under control. Nonetheless, anecdotal evidence suggests the attackers roamed

about in semi-organised groups, even if their precise nature remains obscure. This is probably because of the absence of any formal organisation, particularly any political party, involved in orchestrating the violence. A more likely explanation may be that these groups of attackers were drawn from a variety of informal and semi-organised networks in the hostels and surrounding shack areas.

A key moment in the conflict, and perhaps a turning point, was when a group of attackers marched to Setswetla to launch a raid against the African foreigners living there. When they arrived at the squatter camp, the would-be attackers were met with resistance from local residents. According to Matome Rasetelo, a member of the South African Communist Party and local leader of Setswetla, the marchers said 'they want to take out the *kwerekwere*'. But Setswetla did not allow them. The leaders [of Setswetla] said no, we will take care of our own area and some of the people in Setswetla even helped to bring back some of the stolen goods from the foreigners' places.'[8] Although this was the most resolute example of resistance against the xenophobic attacks, there were countless other instances of local organisations taking very public positions against the violence.

Many individuals also made their mark, not only by denouncing xenophobia, but actively assisting the displaced and traumatised families. One such person is Patience Pashe, a leading member of Women for Peace, who worked tirelessly to comfort, clothe and feed scores of people seeking refuge in the police station.

Nonetheless, at the height of the violence many activists bemoaned the weakness of community organisations and the relative absence of leadership. In the 1980s political leadership was evident and decisive. For a while in the mid-1990s the African National Congress assumed that role. But, it may be argued, the ANC's political hegemony in Alexandra is no longer a source of unity but rather a cause of political fracturing. The township has witnessed a proliferation of competing movements, each representing particular sectors of the community. This is not necessarily a negative development, but during the recent crisis militated against a coherent political response from the community of Alexandra.

However, there are also signs of activists trying to regroup. Members of the SACP, Alexandra Vukuzenzele Crisis Committee (an affiliate of the Anti-Privatisation Forum), churches and welfare organisations, among others, have tried to rally their members to struggle against xenophobia. It is perhaps here, in a reconfiguration of progressive and anti-systemic movements. that a solution lies to xenophobia. But a successful campaign against xenophobia must be combined with continuous campaigns against racism, sexism and ethnic chauvinism (including rejecting the slogan 100% Zulu Boy) and a programme to overcome poverty and deprivation.

BEHIND XENOPHOBIA IN SOUTH AFRICA

POVERTY OR INEQUALITY?

STEPHEN GELB

Many commentators have identified one important set of factors underlying the violence in townships and squatter areas during May to be mounting difficulties faced by poor people. When asked by journalists why the violence had occurred, residents in these areas referred to issues including crime, lack of work, and lack of housing and basic services. Government – in the form of minister Essop Pahad – argued that the violence must be the work of a 'third force' since South Africa has done more than any other developing country for the poor. I would argue that to the extent the violence is linked to the economic circumstances of poor people, it is not the result of poverty *per se*, but rather of inequality. It is surely not simply that people are poor which leads them to attack other poor people, but instead the sense of unfairness engendered by inequality, of being discriminated against, which creates the resentments and hostility towards those perceived, rightly or wrongly, to be better off or to have received preferential treatment.

INEQUALITY IS DISTINCT FROM POVERTY

The main point of this chapter is that poverty and inequality are *distinct* issues: they are *not the same thing* and cannot be addressed by policy as if they are. There is no doubt of course that both poverty and inequality are intractable and deeply-rooted issues in South Africa. In 2005, 47 per cent of the population was in poverty using the widely-agreed poverty line of R322 per capita per month in 2000 prices.[1] This proportion was below the 2000 level of 53 per cent[2], but was nonetheless inordinately high.

Inequality is perhaps even starker. In 2006, the Gini coefficient[3] was officially calculated at 0.73, certainly amongst the two or three highest globally. More revealing perhaps was that the richest 10 per cent of the population received 51 per cent of total household income, while the poorest 10 per cent received a mere 0.2 per cent, the ratio of average income between the two groups thus amounting to a massive 255:1. The richest 20 per cent of the population received 68.8 per cent of the total income, compared with the poorest 20 per cent obtaining only 1.4 per cent, a ratio of 49:1. The poorest 40 per cent of the population received only 6.5 per cent of total household income. An estimated 660 000 households reported no income at all from either work or social grants. [4]

GOVERNMENT HAS ADDRESSED POVERTY BUT NOT INEQUALITY

Pahad's claim that government does a lot for poor people is true as far as it goes. In 2008/9, government will spend 10.7 per

BOTH POVERTY AND INEQUALITY ARE INTRACTABLE AND DEEPLY-ROOTED ISSUES IN SOUTH AFRICA.

cent of its non-interest expenditure on social security grants, an amount of R 70.73 billion, equivalent to 3.3 per cent of gross domestic product. These grants are provided to 12.4 million direct recipients, about a quarter of the population, and augment the welfare of a lot more people once household dependents are included. The number of recipients grew by 11.8 per cent per annum between 2004 and 2008. Even in Gauteng, the richest province, grants reach 1.45 million recipients, about one-sixth of the population.[5]

The total income from social grants as reported by households in 2005/6 was R56.8 billion, equivalent to 6.1 per cent of gross household income. But amongst households in the lowest income decile, grant income was about 75 per cent of household income, and in the second-lowest decile, about 70 per cent.[6]

Other transfers can be added to social grants, such as the free basic water allowance, access to which has increased from 66 per cent of the population in 2004 to a projected 82 per cent this year – 5.25 million more people have been given access to the water allowance in the past four years and another 4.6 million will gain access over the next three years.

Grants and free transfers of goods and services such as the basic water allowance supplement poor people's current incomes and in this way do indeed play a crucial role in alleviating poverty by supporting poor households' consumption. The inequality data reported above incorporates the receipt of social grants (though not publicly provided goods and services), suggesting that the transfer of these resources has not addressed inequality at all. Instead, many measures of inequality suggest it has worsened during the past decade.

ASSET CREATION TO ADDRESS INEQUALITY HAS BEEN INEFFECTIVE

Comparative experience suggests that inequality can only be addressed by transferring assets or building assets, that is, wealth embodied in forms which make it possible to earn income not only today, but in the future. Ownership of assets such as land, education and skills or housing provides poor people with *prospects,* and gives them hope for their future.

In contrast to its income transfer programmes, government's asset transfer and asset building programmes have not succeeded very well. One reason is that these programmes differ from income-supplementing programmes not only in what they provide (higher potential consumption versus higher potential future earnings) to their recipients – that is, on the 'demand side' – but also in the process through which the provision is made, that is, on the 'supply side'.

In the case of income-supplementing grant programmes, the recipients are individuals or individual households and the transaction between provider and recipient is relatively simple: not continuous but intermittent (monthly payments of cash or into bank accounts) and via a link that is fairly easily created and requires little maintenance from the supply side (registration of the recipient and data capture). These features mean that these programmes do not require substantial capacity either from the government agency responsible for managing their provision or from the recipients. For all that there have been problems of corruption and access difficulties for some recipients, the programmes have been largely successful.

In the case of asset-creation programmes, on the other hand, the recipients or consumers are *collective* – 'communities'

– while the transaction between provider and recipient(s) is necessarily either continuous over a long period of time, as in education, or complemented by a range of other services to create a 'package' which is necessary for the produced asset to be of high quality, as in housing provision or land reform. In other words, in asset-development processes, the transaction between provider and recipient is complex and requires substantial capacities on *both* sides.

In some of these programmes, such as land reform, lack of finance has been a major problem. But this does not apply to education, where overall spending has increased by about 2.25 per cent annually in real (inflation-adjusted) terms between 1995 and 2006. Education spending per pupil was equalised across races in the Western Cape province after 1994, substantially narrowing pupil-teacher ratios between races. But the overall matric pass rate dropped up to 2002, and the correlation between race and pass rate remained very strong.[7] Forty per cent of schools still did not have adequate classroom facilities or electrification, while 49 per cent were inadequately supplied with textbooks.[8] In other words, the improvement in equality of educational *inputs* has been of limited scope, and equality in *outcomes* has not improved.

It remains extremely difficult for poor black people to acquire education to use as an asset to leverage their engagement in the economy – jobs, business opportunities and so on – and produce future income. The inability to leverage education and its resulting low quality as an asset is also in part the result of the absence of complementary policies, in areas such as facilitation of job search, apprenticeship and wage dispersion.

IT REMAINS EXTREMELY DIFFICULT FOR POOR BLACK PEOPLE TO ACQUIRE EDUCATION TO USE AS AN ASSET TO LEVERAGE THEIR ENGAGEMENT IN THE ECONOMY.

As Melinda Silverman and Tanya Zack argue in this volume, a lack of complementary reforms is also found in housing, where the focus has been heavily on meeting quantitative targets. The African National Congress promised in 1994 to build a million houses by 1999, and this target was reached by 2000. By 2003, 1.4 million houses had been built and by 2008, 2.6 million.[9] Without diminishing the magnitude of this achievement, there remains an acknowledged shortage of 2.1 million houses. The programme has been criticised for subsidies that are low by international standards and even more strongly for underplaying the diversity of housing demand and the need to locate housing development in the context of broader processes of community development. As with education, there has been little improvement in housing *outcomes*, even though *outputs* in both have increased very considerably.

INEQUALITY NEEDS SPECIFIC POLICY ACTION

For inequality to be reduced, we need to stop identifying it with, indeed reducing it to, poverty, and start addressing them as separate, if linked, issues. We need to maintain the poverty reduction measures which are in place, and even supplement them. But inequality needs to become a priority in its own right. For this to happen, policy must implement change not only at the bottom end of the income and wealth distribution but throughout, that is, also at the top end. Focusing only on the poor will not address inequality – we need to focus on the rich also. This is *not* intended to imply a straight transfer of assets – confiscating from the rich to give to the poor. It is widely recognised that this is not sustainable, even if it were politically possible.

Instead what is needed is to make inequality the *political* priority in a clear and explicit manner. Doing so would have several implications. First, it would imply a fundamental shift in the criteria for allocating government resources. At present, lack of finance is not a constraint on government, but a re-prioritisation of public funding towards asset-creation programmes would send a strong signal as to government's changed priorities.

For example, national government allocated an amount of R19.4 billion over four years to build and renovate stadiums for the World Cup in 2010. Re-directing this money to addressing inequality or poverty is not going to eliminate these problems. Nonetheless, a rough estimate of the opportunity cost of the World Cup is 90 000 additional new houses per year, over and above the 225 000 new houses per year planned for the four-year period to 2010. The question which needs to be asked is: what is our priority as a society – the World Cup or 90 000 houses a year for four years? This sort of choice needs to be made more explicit and discussed more thoroughly if we are to repair the social fabric and avoid future upheavals like those witnessed in May 2008.

It is also clear that the World Cup will absorb a dispro-portionately large share of the time and attention of senior civil servants and political leadership over the next two years. Thus even more important than shifting money would be a re-allocation of government's human and organisational resources to asset-creation policies. Putting its best people onto the school system, the health care system, housing and community infrastructure delivery would surely lead to improved performance.

WHAT IS NEEDED IS TO MAKE **INEQUALITY** THE POLITICAL PRIORITY IN A CLEAR AND EXPLICIT MANNER.

WHAT IS OUR PRIORITY AS A SOCIETY?

The sort of re-thinking of policy and growth priorities which is needed will not come about easily. In countries where lower inequality has been successfully prioritised, it has generally been the result of pressure from a political alliance between the poor and the middle class.

Historically, there are two common reasons for the middle class to ally with the poor. The first is cultural or religious solidarity, as in post-Franco Spain, and the second is recognition of the destabilising effects of inequality in the long run, as in post-Pinochet Chile. The middle class have more to lose than the wealthy from the consequences of inequality, whether political instability linked with the rise of populism or indeed xenophobia, or economic instability due to investor uncertainty. Conversely the middle class has more to gain from economic growth that produces equitable outcomes for working people and the marginalised. As President Thabo Mbeki's 'two nations, two economies' metaphor underlines, economic citizenship is a foundation stone of the shared identity and belonging underlying the 'imagined community' which is the nation (in Benedict Anderson's evocative phrase).

The middle class, or at least significant segments of it, has an essential role in the political, social and cultural processes of nation-building, and black journalists, teachers, writers, lawyers, civil servants, political representatives, activists (including labour leaders) and others are taking a lead in this. But neither these groups, nor the rapidly growing numbers of black managers, small business owners and professionals – many only one generation removed from economic hardship – have expressed themselves clearly on broader economic policy issues (as distinct from black economic empowerment and affirmative action).

If the black middle class is to find its full political voice, the still-larger white middle class has yet to cross the racial divide and embrace the nation-building project. Neither group was directly affected by the xenophobic attacks of May 2008, but for both groups, the fear of being targeted in future violence was real. The issue therefore is whether they will respond to the xenophobia as a threat, and erect higher walls between themselves and the poor, or respond to it as an opportunity to build bridges to the poor and address the challenge of inequality in South Africa.

RELATIVE DEPRIVATION, SOCIAL INSTABILITY AND CULTURES OF ENTITLEMENT

DEVAN PILLAY

The horrific nature of unprovoked attacks on poor people purely on the basis of their nationality makes dispassionate sociological analysis difficult. Nevertheless, despite the emotion, fear and anger at society's descent into barbarism, we need to step back and ask the sober questions: 'Why?' 'What is happening?'

There is, of course, a range of causal factors at play here. These require detailed investigation to isolate the precise triggers for each flare-up in the different parts of the country. A simple focus on 'xenophobia' as an issue of 'identity' ('South Africans hate foreigners' or 'South Africans hate African foreigners') is misleading. A sociological approach immediately subjects the notion of identity to an examination of its complex social determinants. More often than not, inter-related factors of socio-economic class, power and access to resources come to the fore.

I argue that in these flare-ups, where poor people viciously attacked other poor people, class inequality as a systemic problem of uneven development (abundance/scarcity, wealth/poverty, stuffed/starved, insider/outsider, power/powerlessness, empowerment/disempowerment) lay at the root of the violence.

In other words, our post-apartheid 'national democratic revolution', despite its redistributive discourse ('the people shall share'), has unleashed a socio-economic system of *market violence* against the majority of the population, in line with global so-called 'best practice'. The victims of this violence, unable to recognise or reach the real perpetrators or beneficiaries of this violence, have, as often happens, lashed out at those closest to them. Whereas in other instances this might have taken a gendered form (men beating their wives), or an ethnic form (so-called 'tribal clashes'), in this instance the convenient scapegoats were easily recognisable foreign nationals – particularly those with houses, jobs or small businesses.

In the midst of this uprising, 'criminals', as a recent report suggests, stepped in to loot, and may have been behind copycat flare-ups that spread around the country. Of course the 'criminals' themselves are the products of marginality; victims of the systemic violence who have learnt the law of the jungle, where the only morality is survival at all costs.

While researchers quibble over whether the pervasive blight of poverty has marginally decreased or increased since 1994, no-one disputes that inequality continues to increase at an alarming rate. Rising inequality breeds perverse cultures of entitlement and experiences of relative deprivation, which lie at the root of social instability.

CLASS INEQUALITY AS A SYSTEMIC PROBLEM OF UNEVEN
DEVELOPMENT LAY AT THE ROOT OF THE VIOLENCE.

CULTURES OF ENTITLEMENT

It has become common in elite and policy circles to talk of a 'culture of entitlement' when arguing against extending welfare benefits (i.e. sharing the social surplus) to poor people who cannot find jobs because of jobless growth. 'These people do not want to work. They just sit back and expect the state to provide for them' is a popular refrain in business, government and professional forums around the world.

For example, this argument has been used repeatedly in South Africa against the extension of child support grants to single mothers, on the basis that young women are deliberately becoming pregnant to obtain these grants, and then spend the meagre sum on 'hairdos, alcohol and boyfriends',[1] while leaving their mother or granny to look after their child or children. No evidence, just a few anecdotes, and with the aid of a pliable mass media almost everyone repeats it like a mantra.

This is not surprising, given the hegemonic ideological discourse that idolises the market and demonises the redistributive state and a mobilised civil society. When decoded this discourse is actually saying that the rich minority who, through fair means or foul, accumulate vast wealth are good – they deserve what they get; while the poor majority who need assistance and social solidarity are bad – they deserve what *they* get.

Luckily, in South Africa a number of investigations by different, independent research bodies have concluded that there is no evidence of widespread abuse of the child support grant. In fact, it has become essential to support the most basic survival activities in many households. But if we did not have a sympathetic minister of social development to commission this research, the mantra of 'entitlement' would have prevailed, and the grants would have been slashed or abolished, further tearing apart our social fabric.

What then, are the real 'cultures of entitlement'? I suggest that there are two:

CULTURE OF ENTITLEMENT TYPE 1:
ILLEGITIMATE EXPECTATIONS

This struck me the other day when I met the wife of an ex-activist and she said, 'My husband bought me this sports car and I deserve it'. This is what we call conspicuous consumption, and the wife, a former radical activist herself, was completely unapologetic. 'I *deserve* it,' she said emphatically. Her husband has the wealth so she is entitled to spend it.

I felt too sick to press her further, but if I did she would probably plead relative deprivation, and refer to those who earn and spend far more than what she and her husband do – like Whitey Basson, the CEO of Shoprite-Checkers, who 'earned' approximately R60 million in 2005. The *Business Day's* Rob Rose[2] said he deserved it, because he 'earned' so much profit for the company's shareholders. Relatively speaking, compared to CEOs in the United States or Europe, he is underpaid, goes the market logic. The company's workers, on the other hand, earn a pittance, but they are not forced to work. In a sea of unemployment, you take what you can get. Impeccable, simple market logic, devoid of the messiness of morality. The working class, long stripped of access to the means of subsistence, is free – to work or to starve.

Of course, within this context of expanding inequality, another illegitimate culture of entitlement takes root: criminality. If the socially legitimate route to survival is blocked, the poor may resort to illegal means to survive. Within a broader culture of corruption, greed and the idolisation of accumulation and consumption, criminals may not stop at crime for mere survival, but might also steal, assault and murder in order to mimic the lifestyles of those at the apex of greed.

Others may not use violence as such, but will nevertheless break the rules in an orgy of primitive accumulation in order to catch up with established white wealth, the looters from the apartheid era. It is the law of the jungle, *tata ma chance*, or take what you can get, according to the rules or in violation of the rules. *Business Day* editor Peter Bruce,[3] eager to preserve the system, says let them loot, and then give them amnesty, because we need to grow a black upper-middle class fast. In other words, to further 'deracialise' the pigs gorging at the trough.

CULTURE OF ENTITLEMENT TYPE 2:
LEGITIMATE EXPECTATIONS, UNMET BASIC NEEDS

The vast majority cry: 'I deserve nutritious food, clean water, decent shelter, warmth, adequate security.' These are basic human rights, enshrined in our Constitution, to which all are entitled but which are being violated every day, every minute, every second. This country and the world grow enough food to feed everyone twice over, but half the population starves, and even more are malnourished. Yet there is a muted public outcry and no state of emergency, except when the people rise up and revolt. And, in their desperation, without proper organisation under a progressive leadership, they can be revolting.

IT IS THE LAW OF THE JUNGLE

TATA MA CHANCE

TAKE WHAT YOU CAN GET
ACCORDING TO THE RULES OR
IN VIOLATION OF THE RULES.

RELATIVE DEPRIVATION

It is not poverty *per se* that causes revolutions or uprisings, but relative deprivation. In other words, rising expectations in a context where only some, the insiders, have their needs met and a tiny minority of those insiders are getting filthy rich. Over a decade ago, our current deputy president, then deputy minister of trade and industry, declared: 'Blacks must not be afraid to be filthy rich.'[4] That is how we started off our democracy. The main content of our 'development' trajectory has been about merging a newly formed black elite into the dominant white economic elite. Under the rubric of the 'national democratic revolution', those with their hand on the levers of power have openly declared: 'We did not struggle to be poor.'

This, of course, is the same depressing story across post-colonial Africa, Latin America and Asia (with a few notable exceptions). A new political elite, using revolutionary phraseology, scrambling over each other to touch the hands of the economically dominant ex-colonial elite and be accepted into the club of global super-insiders. This is what some[5] in South Africa call the '1996 class project', except that it began in the late 1980s in exile, intensified after 1994, and has now broken out into open warfare amongst thieves. When the new ruling party leadership,[6] stocked with a new set of *lumpen bourgeoisie*, say: 'It is now our turn', or 'The people shall share in the country's wealth', it should be clear who 'our' or 'the people' really are.

Given this naked display of self-enrichment, what is the reaction of the outsiders – the marginalised, the unemployed, the informalised and the working poor? Most of the time their discontent is subdued, and resentment bubbles beneath the

OF COURSE THIS IS A GLOBAL PHENOMENON, NOT PECULIARLY SOUTH AFRICAN.

surface. Where they are organised into progressive trade unions and social movements of various kinds, then the demands of outsiders can be put forward in a disciplined way to achieve a clear objective. When it is not properly organised, it is angry, desperate and at times expressed in barbaric ways, as we saw over the two dark weeks of May.

Of course this is a global phenomenon, not peculiarly South African. Where there are rising expectations, growing inequality and relative deprivation, in the absence of a coherent political movement to channel that energy into effective mobilisation for social change, this anger can be woefully misdirected. Fuelled by a xenophobic tabloid press, it can be deadly. Politicians have been either indifferent to the rising xenophobia, or have themselves fuelled it. Years ago I heard African National Congress councillors in Yeoville talking about 'these foreigners taking jobs'. To be sure, not all politicians espouse this, but too many have. In addition there has for years been police brutality against African foreigners, including extortion and victimisation. In that context, we are asking for trouble.

The Italian Marxist Antonio Gramsci, writing about capitalist crisis, characterised it as a period in which the old is dying (and it's taking a long time to die) while the new struggles to be born and in this 'interregnum, a great variety of morbid symptoms appear'.[7] We are now in such an interregnum between the old and the new struggling to be formed. Gruesome, grizzly, crazed, mindless violence of a few, stepping into barbarism. Nevertheless, they carry the views of a vast number of poor, impoverished people who, in the competition for 'scarce' resources, believe that 'they're taking our jobs' or that they're 'taking our houses'.

OTHERWISE WE WILL ALL, EVENTUALLY,
DESCEND INTO BARBARISM.

There is a deep underlying problem in this country (and the world) and the solution is not the narrow policy prescription of the alleviation of poverty. Firstly, given the world's resources and our own country's resources, we must talk of the elimination of poverty. But secondly, to achieve that we must also focus on what Wolfgang Sachs calls the alleviation of wealth.[8] We must see how these two are dialectically interlinked. We need to build a counter-hegemonic movement in this country, which includes those of us in the middle classes committed to social justice, as part of the growing global counter-hegemonic movement against the systemic problem of inequality, poverty and destitution on the one hand, and mind-boggling wealth on the other.

Otherwise we will all, eventually, descend into barbarism.

VIOLENCE, CONDEMNATION, AND THE MEANING OF LIVING IN SOUTH AFRICA

LOREN B LANDAU

Refugees, asylum seekers, immigrants, illegals, border jumpers, displacees, Nigerians, aliens, *amakwerekwere* have long been on South Africans' minds. For many they are primarily groups to be feared, disdained, occasionally pitied, often exploited and seen as a threat to the country's wealth and health. The country's government and much of its civil society has long turned a blind eye to foreigners' systematic marginalisation, mass deportation (close to 300 000 people in 2007) and the ever more rapid and rabid murders at the hands of the country's citizenry.

When the government did react to violence against foreigners, its responses were two-faced: chastising communities for their intolerance while accelerating arrests and removals.[1] In a nationally broadcast speech on 25 May, President Thabo Mbeki encouraged South Africans to '... build on the tradition of many decades of integrating our foreign guests within our communities'.[2] Given the history of exploitation, alienation and expulsion, it is hard to imagine where he (or anyone else) got the idea that government or citizens have ever promoted the peaceful integration of migrants into South African society.

But my concern here is not with the long-term disregard for migrants' rights and welfare. Nor is it to condemn the initial denialism of crisis or the tardy and ineffective efforts to help those who were violently displaced.[3] Rather, this piece considers what the responses by South African citizens and institutions reveal about being from and living in South Africa.

In particular, I am interested in two puzzling reactions to the violence. The first is the uncharacteristically startling reaction from civil society – particularly middle class South African society – and the normative content of that reaction. The second is the strange dichotomy officials made between xenophobic and criminal motivations and their insistence that what took place was criminal.[4]

As a moment of crisis when the security of residents' bodies, possessions and values came under question, the violence serves both to destroy and create. Speaking in the most general and aggregated terms, the attacks have helped generate three incompatible views of life in South Africa. The first is a renewed (if circumscribed) commitment to cosmopolitan nationalism by elements of South Africa's middle class and government elite: to respect the rights of all living in the country. This is countered by what is undoubtedly a far more prevalent perspective: killing foreigners may not be right, but South Africa must remain the domain of those who have sprung from its soil.

UNLESS WE ADDRESS THE ETHICAL AND PRACTICAL TENSIONS VIOLENCE WILL ALWAYS BE JUST AROUND THE CORNER.

Removed from debates over who belongs sit the migrants themselves. Rejecting aspirations of or claims to membership, they are further distancing themselves from the citizenry. In so doing they claim rights to be in South Africa but not part of it. Unless we address the ethical and practical tensions reflected in these views over how we live together and relate to our neighbours, violence will always be just around the corner.

Before exploring the reactions and the competing visions of South Africa they represent, it is worth noting two ironies that were undoubtedly lost on the third-force masterminds behind 5/11. First, by drastically reducing remittances from South Africa to Zimbabwe, the murder and displacement of migrants may have killed one of the last lifelines to our northern neighbours. Without even the meagre material migrants in South Africa provide to families in Zimbabwe – soap, cash, cooking oil – more people will starve and others will flee. Rather than staying home and living off South African-made products, many of them will undoubtedly end up in South Africa. Once here, they are likely to stay for the foreseeable future.

Second, while few of the foreigners displaced by the violence had ever accessed state support or services in the past (even when legally entitled to them),[5] tens of thousands ended up in state-run shelters where they were almost fully dependent on the state for months. If the South African government eventually establishes semi-permanent camps to protect foreigners from the citizenry, refugees will finally receive the free food and shelter that South Africans have long accused them of purloining. Even if the international community picked up the tab, the lost labour, taxes, investments and moral authority will eventually cost South Africa both cash and jobs.

Turning now to middle class civil society and its uncharacteristically immediate and forceful outrage, in some respects their response is easy to explain. While murder is a daily occurrence and the government regularly displaces South Africans from informal settlements, addressing these sorts of problems requires sustained political critique and engagement. Many have neither the time nor the energy to undertake such campaigns. Others remain wary of criticising the ruling coalition, either out of ideological sympathy or for fear of being publicly condemned.[6]

Moreover, sustained engagement means confronting uncomfortable issues about crime, redistribution, and our willingness to live side by side with a rapidly urbanising – but still desperately poor – citizenry. It is also far easier to support people who are unequivocally victims of violence rather than the poor struggling for survival in not-quite acceptable ways. Paradoxically, the acts levelled against these 'illegal' immigrants have legitimised foreigners' rights and presence in South Africa in a way that their long-standing economic, political and cultural contributions never have. A widely condemned category of freeloaders and criminals is now a group to be pitied and protected.

But I suspect there is a more complex explanation for the rapid awakening of some within the slumbering middle class civil society. With the transition to democracy, many activists went silent, either brought into lucrative government positions or deeply sympathetic to a legitimate government that was clearly committed to righting past injustice. Others simply moved on, content to turn their attention to domestic and material pursuits

WITH THE TRANSITION TO DEMOCRACY, MANY ACTIVISTS WENT SILENT.

now that the key battle was won. However, reticence could only be justified if South African society was becoming more equal and more tolerant. The overt and violent discrimination we witnessed in the middle of May highlights the degree to which the poor remain deeply and inequitably, well, poor. It also reveals that the grander project of social inclusion is far off track. Until it is back on course, more fundamental threats to values and privilege are just below the horizon.

The dangers lying ahead are particularly acute for white and Indian members of the country's middle class. For some, the redistributive impulse implicit in the mobs threatens long-standing positions of privilege. For others – many who support a more radical redistribution agenda – it is the nativism behind the attacks and other more formal political developments[7] that is most disquieting. While it may not immediately threaten middle class lives, it threatens their position in a future South African society. Coupled with anxieties over the presumptive future president Jacob Zuma, and Zimbabwe just up the road, few need to be reminded of what can happen if xenophobic nativism migrates from the streets into mainstream policy. For many, condemning the violence is one way that an economically powerful political minority can protest against that possibility; defending tolerance to migrants already in the country becomes a proxy claim for themselves in a diverse South Africa.

As for government leaders, they clearly share the middle class anxieties over the overt challenges to constitutional values and the rule of law. For those close to President Mbeki, they also worry about their place in South Africa. Undoubtedly, heeding the populist mobs would quickly strip them of the entitlements

FEW NEED TO BE REMINDED OF WHAT CAN HAPPEN IF XENOPHOBIC NATIVISM MIGRATES FROM THE STREETS INTO MAINSTREAM POLICY.

to which they have only just become accustomed. But that does not explain their insistence that the violence was more criminal than xenophobic. Like the middle class whose protests also serve to defend their future in South African society, the motivations for proclaiming criminality are at least in part about protecting officials' domestic and international legitimacy.

One might think that the general corruption, lawlessness, and poverty would already have done irreparable damage to their domestic and international credibility (as it evidently has done among the mobs). But among the politically empowered, the international community, and the poor, the government has successfully hidden behind a language of 'progressive realisation' and 'implementation capacity'. Even crime is packaged as a problem of police transformation, not as a symptom of more fundamental dividing lines within South African society. To the degree that government can code events as criminal, they protect their legitimacy as champions of transformation stymied only by practical challenges and reactionary forces.

Conversely, labelling these as xenophobic attacks threatens officials' international and domestic position as the poster-children for progressive social change. Around the world, people look to the South African miracle and exalt our leaders for their remarkable achievements. Rob them of these achievements and people who are now received as heroes, sit on human rights panels and lecture on South Africa's progress – which is considerable – will be thrown in the basket with the rest of Africa. Despite the rhetoric of pan-Africanism, many South African officials' disdain for what happens elsewhere on the continent means there can, in their eyes, be little worse. Given that many of them also have business interests that depend on South Africa's reputation, there is the added threat to their bank balances.

The reactions and counter-reactions among the mobs, the middle class, government and migrants are helping to cement three visions for life in South Africa. Among the middle classes and government officials, we will likely see increasing cosmopolitanism creeping into the ethical basis of their nationalism. Now that xenophobia has been elevated to the likes of racism, sexism and homophobia, people will be reluctant to speak in overtly nationalistic terms. At the very least, it will reaffirm the idea that South Africa belongs to all who *live* in it. (Although many would prefer to place far greater limits on just who gets the chance to do that.)

Such cosmopolitanism is by no means universal among South African residents. As the violence has shown, many South Africans cling to a deeply territorialised understanding of the South African project. They no longer question that South Africa should become a far more controlled space, or, better yet, an exclusively South African domain. Calls for stronger border controls from the Democratic Alliance, the Human Sciences Research Council, the Institute for Security Studies and even the Institute for Race Relations bespeak a broader process of territorial control linked to a view that South African resources – land, jobs, and grants – must be reserved for those who can claim South African origins or those explicitly approved by them. This may not yet be an ethnic nationalism, but it is an overt assertion of a territorially bound community.[8] For the mobs and those sympathetic to them, the Fanonian violence will go a step further, strengthening the principle that South Africa belongs to all who were *born* in it.

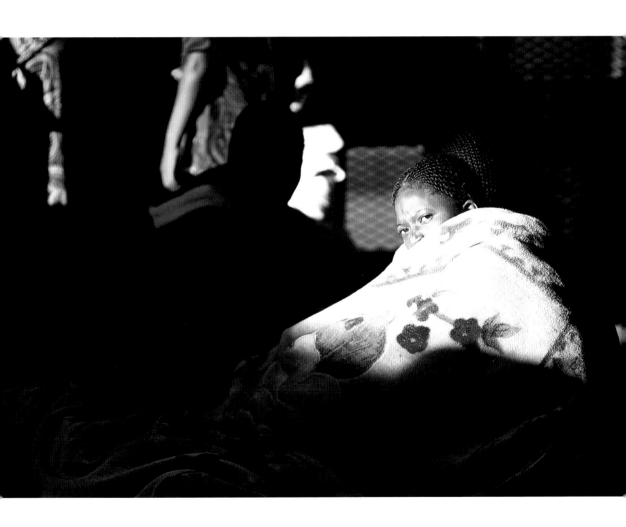

IT MAY NOT BE LONG BEFORE WE HEAR
MORE THAN THE DISTANT ROAR OF BATTLE.

And where does this leave the international migrants? I suspect that South Africa will increasingly host alien populations that are shaping their own idioms of transient superiority. Clinging to the status afforded those belonging to the mobile classes, they will continue to sit just outside (or above) South African society, emotionally orienting themselves elsewhere. Instead of seeking integration and recognition within South Africa's society and politics, many will strive for a kind of usufruct rights: a form of self-exclusion that is at least partially compatible with the kind of social and political marginalisation they have experienced.[9] To their potential detriment, this lack of commitment to South Africa may only further enrage those already prepared to do them harm.

The divisions between self-exclusion, cosmopolitan citizenship and ethnic nationalism are dangerous ones – not only as differences in values, but because they map so closely with class, race and nationality. As such, they provide tectonic faults that may result in far greater disruptions. With an increasingly centralised and unpopular political party mandated to span the divides, it may not be long before we hear more than the distant roar of battle.

CROSSING BORDERS

DAVID COPLAN

Interviewed in the *Sunday Independent* (Johannesburg) of 25 May 2008 about the recent attacks on foreign nationals, an unknown 'student' who had participated in the attacks on African immigrants is

> ... adamant that all the problems started at South Africa's borders. They are too porous, are not properly policed and border posts are manned by corrupt officials who let anybody in ... The government must work hard to secure our borders. Home Affairs must be sorted out. We're helping the government, now, to send them back.[1]

While some may wish to argue that we are somehow 'all Africans together', the political facts on the ground are that

South Africa, like any other sovereign national state, has the right to decide which foreign citizens should or should not be admitted at its borders, and under what conditions. The South African government also has the right to pick and choose among applicants for entry or residence on the basis of its own interests, priorities and policies. All countries do this, and some observers, like migration expert Dr Wilmot James, say that South Africa has a responsibility to control its borders as an obligation to the Constitution and the rule of law.[2] Certainly South Africa is not required to accept any number of people either from Africa or anywhere else simply because they are destitute or see better opportunities for themselves here than elsewhere.

An exception to this would be genuine refugees fleeing the immediate threat of violence or imprisonment at home, but the South African government has not shown much enthusiasm for differentiating between economic and political refugees, or for granting legal residence to either category of 'forced migrant'. This confusion has had additional ill effects due to government denials that there are any crises in other African countries or that there is a real category of 'genuine' African political refugees.

The government of South Africa shows little enthusiasm in practice for investing in the effective physical monitoring and control of its land borders. What the student said in the *Sunday Independent* is, by most reports, close to the mark: South African identity is for sale. There is no document, no permit, no identity, no official status that one cannot obtain for the right amount of money. When one sees asylum seekers queuing or even sleeping outside Home Affairs offices, sometimes for days or weeks on end, complaining of not being well served, the attitude within

SOUTH AFRICAN IDENTITY IS FOR SALE.

the department seems to be: 'If they want to be well served, and obtain the legal right to reside here, why are they not willing to pay for the privilege?' The idea that refugees have some *right* to be 'well served' – given access to the resource of South African residence – does not really have much 'purchase'.

Whether in downtown Johannesburg or down at the borders, it's the same sort of officials with the same kind of attitude, following the same script and rationale. Before 1994, South Africa's border posts were run by the old South African Police and they had an interest in protecting the country from the 'terrorists' who they believed were threatening to put a black government into power, so they did a somewhat more effective job. Today, however, Immigration officials have a rather different priority: running our borders as a business. The current state is not really concerned about any 'foreign threat'. Until the recent, embarrassing 'xenophobic' attacks, the principal reason they and the South African Police Service had for controlling or patrolling the borders was to ensure that reasonable numbers of immigrants would pay reasonable (to border officials) unofficial fees to enter and reside in South Africa.

South African identity and residence, legal or illegal, is a cash cow for the people who work in border management. So if you go down to many of the borders and you don't have a legal entry document or passport, you can always use a R100 note as a passport. Granted you cannot just walk in, but you can certainly negotiate entry no matter what your situation. On the border the qualification for joining the Immigration services is a Standard 8 from any South African school. Many lower ranking immigration officials have never read – in fact cannot read – the immigration

regulations that they are supposed to enforce, but they do collect the money from people who need to circumvent them. Regional Immigration Department centres in Bloemfontein or Musina or Pretoria only appear to complain about 'corruption' at the border when more senior officials are not getting their cut of the take down at the border.

The reality is that the state just doesn't see any reason to keep people out, not even when uncounted numbers of Zimbabweans are fleeing the insupportable situation in their country. They can, the government has believed, be safely imposed on the society in general, and left to make their way with their own resources, without services or assistance from the public or the Treasury. While the recent violence – against South African 'others' as well as against non-nationals, it turns out – has forced a change in that belief, there is little likelihood that these events will change things at the border posts.

Of course, under pressure from the dispossessed, there will surely be government announcements of border management reform. But despite such public relations exercises I don't see Home Affairs being 'sorted out' any time soon, because there is little the government believes it will gain from doing so. The government wants a healthy return on its investments, and it sees little in the way of revenue that might repay an expenditure of, let us say, R200 million to reform and regularise control at the borders. Indeed such measures might actually reduce revenues, as the money that flows from the illicit sale of entrances would surely then be harder to safely extract.

The police, who are also at the border, but more importantly who conduct the raids that constitute internal borders here in Johannesburg, spend a very high proportion of their time chasing around after what they call 'illegal aliens' in order to arrest them and shake them down.[3] While many immigrants pay the police and officials at Home Affairs to be left in peace, tens of thousands of people from neighbouring states are deported every year and of course they come back. This will continue despite the student's claim that 'We're [the violent mobs] helping the government, now, to send them back', because the immigrants and their families back home must still find a livelihood, and South Africa still provides their best chance.

That doesn't concern the government particularly, because if these would-be immigrants come back, South Africans can continue in the not unprofitable occupation of shaking them down. We have seen on SABC TV's *Special Assignment* what happens at Booysens Police Station, where arrested undocumented immigrants are made to pay for the privilege of carrying on with their lives in Johannesburg. One has to pay for the right to be here, unless of course you're a South African, in which case, they can still shake you down.

If you come from Limpopo and you don't have an ID because you have no birth certificate and live far from Home Affairs offices, and you only speak Tsonga and you come to Johannesburg to find a job, you can be picked up for being a suspected Mozambican and indeed, even if you've never been to Mozambique, be sent 'back' there. Now you are truly a foreigner in a country you've never seen, without any documents, and you are forced to negotiate your way through the wilds of the Kruger Park or, illegally somehow, back into the country of which you are actually a citizen without any assistance. This does happen.

TENS OF THOUSANDS OF PEOPLE FROM NEIGHBOURING STATES
ARE DEPORTED EVERY YEAR AND OF COURSE THEY COME BACK.

WHEN YOU WATCH A UNIFORMED OFFICIAL AT THE BORDER POST WINDOWS LOOKING AT YOUR PASSPORT AND TYPING AWAY, THERE IS ACTUALLY NO INFORMATION ON THE SCREEN EXCEPT WHETHER OR NOT YOU HAVE A VALID TRAVEL DOCUMENT. OFFICIALS CLAIM THAT THE TERMINALS ARE CONNECTED TO THE SAPS MOVEMENT CONTROL SYSTEM. **THEY ARE NOT.**

As in the case of many among the 21 South African citizens who were killed in the recent mob violence, one is innocent until proven Venda or Shangaan.

What would it take to 'sort out' Home Affairs? It would require tens of millions of rands for the upgrading of infrastructure, for updated and expanded technology, record keeping, and data management, for improved training and a higher level of basic education of staff, for effective corruption control and the reduction of smuggling and other crime.

As it stands, the actual technology and data now available to Immigration officials at the border posts is hopelessly limited, and what they do have is ineffectively used. When you watch a uniformed official at the border post windows looking at your passport and typing away, there is actually no information on the screen except whether or not you have a valid travel document. Officials claim that the terminals are connected to the SAPS Movement Control System. They are not.

On a typical day during the peak season in December, 16 000 people cross Maseru Bridge into Lesotho. If I am one of them I will get my passport stamped, at some cost in time and inconvenience, by both South African and Lesotho officials. But as far as the computer is concerned, there is no indication of whether 16 000 different people have crossed or if Professor Coplan has crossed 16 000 times. If you are deported, you can go around the building and come straight back to South Africa on a 14-day visitor's visa. There is no record available to those people tap-tapping on the computer that you have just been deported, stolen the car you are driving, committed a crime or are wanted in South Africa or Lesotho.

If the South African government were to make a credible effort to remedy this situation, it would require some imperative for doing so – and where would the revenue come from that would repay this effort? They are not going to allocate significant resources simply because migration experts like Dr James consider that they have an 'obligation' to do so, nor to please the above-mentioned less-than-useless 'student' who, unlike most undocumented immigrants, does no work, pays no taxes except VAT, and still expects to receive government services and assistance. If one is to insist that the government spend all these millions and effectively kill the border business that is generating salary supplementations for staff and income for hundreds of individual unofficial 'border entrepreneurs', where would the economic or political benefit come from that would justify such an investment?

The final disincentive is the reality that illegal or undocumented entry into South Africa would continue even if this investment were made. If the mighty United States, similarly faced with illegal immigration by vastly poorer neighbours, can spend billions of dollars to secure its southern border without success, then South Africa surely has neither the will nor the resources to succeed. So it makes little practical sense for the current South African state to attempt to stop undocumented immigration in any genuinely effective way.

The recent looting, destruction, and violence visited by poor young men in informal settlements upon their defenceless neighbours, citizens and non-citizens alike, will provide the impetus for a kind of rhetorical reform and symbolic control at our borders, producing official statements, workshops, policy

ILLEGAL OR UNDOCUMENTED ENTRY INTO SOUTH AFRICA WOULD CONTINUE EVEN IF THIS INVESTMENT WERE MADE.

documents and rafts of regulations (which serve only to increase the corruption that follows upon the increased inconvenience of circumventing them) intended for domestic political consumption.

Yet, in concluding, I would in principle agree with Dr James and suggest that improved border management is both worthwhile and possible. There is considerable value for our national life and institutions in attempting to end the uncontrolled outright sale of South African identity and right of residence, and at the same time to open our doors – in a properly documented but responsive fashion – to those immigrants that we have every reason and responsibility to welcome.

POLICING XENOPHOBIA—
XENOPHOBIC POLICING

A CLASH OF LEGITIMACY

JULIA HORNBERGER

As the first images and news reports about the outbreak of violence against migrants broke, it was striking how many migrants fled to police stations for shelter and protection. After all they were seeking sanctuary there despite their overwhelming experience of the police officer as the taunter of migrants, the one who habitually exploited migrants' informal, often legally compromised and vulnerable status, through deportation, extortion and exploitation. But there they were, knocking at the gates of Alex police station, huddling together and demanding entrance at Cleveland police station, squatting in the courtyard, halls and barracks of Jeppe police station. It couldn't have been more incongruous.

In trying to understand what happened in this moment in which migrants sought and were granted refuge at the police stations, I argue that the usual kind of complicity in the xenophobic sentiments which underpin and are being reproduced through everyday police practice was suspended in favour of a policing of what could be read as a more cosmopolitan and inclusive order.

Surely, one could simply see it as further testimony of the migrants' terrible fate and desperation: having to seek protection from those who abuse them, facing a terrible choice between two evils. Yet I would argue that by arriving on the doorsteps of the police station the migrants were also appealing to a different kind of police, a police which would at least protect their right to life.

And the amazing thing was that the police took up the challenge. They opened their gates and let the refugees in and let them stay. They even promised them that nobody would be deported, a cunning move that police had previously used when a similar but far less publicised incident took place in January at the Laudium police station.[1] This was a momentary inclusive act by the police. Somehow, in this moment, a practice of human rights had been invoked and enacted; some form of a just state had come to the fore.

Why did this happen? Was it the sheer numbers of desperate people? Was it that their desperation appealed to a very basic, if not always apparent, sense of duty of police officers, namely the duty to protect the lives of innocent people, whoever they may be? Was it, perhaps, that the police are not so 'xenophobic' after all? Or was it merely the police's awareness of media attention?

There is anecdotal evidence that police officers even went beyond their call of duty. At one of the police stations, for example, police officers set up a television set in the hall in which displaced migrants were staying. Other police officers went out

WHY DID THIS HAPPEN? WAS IT THE SHEER NUMBERS OF DESPERATE PEOPLE?

of their way to bring in mattresses so that migrants did not have to sleep on the chilly concrete floors. Whatever the reasons, it was a moment in which the relationship between police and migrants was reconstituted as one of securing protection and realising a sense of a humanitarian justice.

I was even led to think that these acts could mean that this terrible moment of the violent attacks on migrants had produced something good; that this refashioned relationship between police and migrants could even help with the reintegration of migrants. Maybe this quite intimate moment of the enactment of human rights and more so of a relationship of hospitality in the face of inhospitality would leave its mark and last beyond the moment.

But what was I thinking? While the willingness of volunteers was still fervent and the donated goods were still flowing *en masse* from concerned and outraged citizens to the dislocated people, a good friend of mine had a revealing conversation with the commissioner of a police station which had opened its gates to the refugees.[2] The story she related to me forced me to reconsider the incidents above in a different light.

She was helping out as one of the many volunteers at the police station and she had approached the station commissioner about the rapidly deteriorating sanitary conditions for the migrants at the station. The conversation took an interesting turn. It became an occasion for the station commissioner to express his exasperation and anxiety about housing the migrants at his station. He made it clear to her that he wanted them gone as soon as possible. For him, the migrants' departure – no matter if they had a place to go to or not – was more than overdue.

AND THE AMAZING THING WAS THAT
THE POLICE TOOK UP THE CHALLENGE.

Initially, he brought up the station's maintenance budget and what it was costing him to house the migrants, saying that he would soon run out of money or have no means left for the rest of the year. But then, switching to a seemingly unrelated aspect, deeper concerns and anxieties surfaced. He told her that it was only recently that the police officers of his station had managed to built up a relationship of trust with the community; it was only of late that policing could be carried out with some level of co-operation from the community and that this kind of policing was bearing fruit in terms of their fight against crime. However, he continued, if he were to be seen to be housing and protecting migrants any longer, all the trust which had been painstakingly built up would erode again.

Then, in what seemed like yet another abrupt move, he switched to a story of his experiences as a black police officer in Thembisa during the 1980s. He related to my friend an account of how he had been apprehended during the unrests by some of the protesters who had made him eat faeces. At first it seemed rather incoherent the way he skipped from one story to the next but as we reflected on it, it made perfect sense. The way he was speaking, moving from one topic to another without taking along the one who was listening, clearly was a form of traumatic speech. What he was doing here was going back to a traumatic memory, the memory of what it meant to 'be on the wrong side of the community'. Having to protect the migrants and to house them at his station had the power to collapse the past within the present and in that move to be once again on the wrong side of the community.

The comments and reactions of the station commissioner suggest that what is being pitched here against each other are two versions of legitimacy based on two different versions of order which the police are supposed to serve. It also suggests that this clash of orders is a very real one for the police. In the early transformation of the police, immediately after the 1994 election, the issue of the lack of legitimacy and trust by the population in the police stood central. The community policing approach, which foregrounded immediate accountability of police to the local population, was envisaged as a means of regaining people's trust. And with trust would come co-operation, and with co-operation would come a more efficient form of crime fighting.

It is one thing to say that police officers hold xenophobic attitudes – attitudes here denoting a form of world-view, an issue of consciousness and interiority which then comes to inform practice. But perhaps it is rather through the panacea of community policing and the kind of close-up interaction of immediate accountability between police and community which it propagates that has produced a practice which demands xenophobic attitudes from the police; perhaps it is the genuine impulse and desire of police officers to become a better police force, that police officers have come to accept xenophobic attitudes, and latitude in the face of attacks on foreigners, as best practice.

Let me explain: Policing is characterised by the employment of discretion. Discretion is situated, for example, in the need to interpret an ambiguous and complex reality to fit the delineated categories of the law. Also, good policing is often understood as being the ability to arbitrate in conflicts to keep the peace, rather than to enforce the law indiscriminately. When to keep peace and when to enforce the law again is largely an issue of

THIS CLASH OF ORDERS IS A VERY REAL ONE FOR THE POLICE.

OR MAYBE TRUST AND POLICE ARE NOT REALLY TWO THINGS WHICH SHOULD GO TOGETHER TOO CLOSELY.

police discretion. Community policing implies that discretion is applied in such a way as to gain the trust of community.

It is this triad of trust-discretion-community which can potentially produce legitimacy for the police and the state on a local level, but it might be exactly that which also produces – with the complicity of the police – brutal forms of local justice and vengeance. Especially if the latter are sentiments and expressions of people who feel disempowered and left out of economic prosperity and make sense of it by blaming both real and elusive 'others' for their situation. In such a constellation, human rights appear as the taunting mockery of a distant order to which they have no entry ticket.

So what does that mean? Perhaps it means that it is time to disentangle the police from too much community policing. Perhaps the notion of autonomy of the police has to be enhanced and the police should rather gain trust not from 'the community' alone but from *all* people being policed. Or maybe trust and police are not really two things which should go together too closely. More importantly, it is apparent – again – that policing is ultimately a political act and that we ask ourselves whose order is being policed, and whose order should be policed.

HOUSING DELIVERY, THE URBAN CRISIS AND XENOPHOBIA

MELINDA SILVERMAN AND TANYA ZACK

The xenophobic attacks that took place at the end of May in Johannesburg were located in particular spaces in the city: in shack settlements, in the vicinity of hostels, and in inner city suburbs. These are housing environments that have been neglected by the state. They are characterised by severe overcrowding, deteriorating services, high levels of poverty, rampant unemployment, ongoing racial segregation and the daily struggles of poor people forced to compete with one another for increasingly scarce resources. In these places ethnicity and national identity were used to legitimise the wholesale theft of people's houses. In this way the housing crisis was inextricably linked to the xenophobia crisis.

The problem is not that the state has neglected housing delivery, but that the state has tragically misinterpreted housing need. There is a fundamental mismatch between the government's modernist vision underpinning housing policy and the messy, postmodern reality of today's urban milieu.

The underlying assumptions of this modernist paradigm are full employment, social stability, aspirations to orderliness, impermeable nation states, nuclear family arrangements, and homogeneity. In contrast the postmodern conditions of our time include high unemployment, mobility and migrancy,[1] intensified trans-national flows, new household arrangements that are very rarely nuclear, and hybridity.

STATE HOUSING DELIVERY

Housing delivery has been one of the strengths of the new government. Some 2.6 million houses have been delivered since 1994, making housing one of the state programmes benefiting the greatest number of people.

The most visible manifestation of state housing delivery is in the form of 'RDP' houses,[2] orderly rows of standardised, mass-produced units on the peripheries of our cities.[3] In these environments, there may have been enough money to deliver the housing unit, but not enough to build garden fences, pave the sidewalks, or provide social facilities, schools or clinics. Numerical targets have been emphasised at the expense of location, condemning these settlements to remote urban areas and distant rural towns. In many instances this location is selected not to meet livelihood needs for employment and infrastructure but because delivering housing is a form of political patronage.

Access to this housing is severely circumscribed. Beneficiaries must have South African residency, have dependents and earn below R3 500 a month. They are expressly forbidden from selling their houses for a period of five years.[4] Houses come with freehold tenure, but the benefit of freehold is dubious in the context of high unemployment, when the ability to move in search of work may be more highly valued than property ownership. Beneficiaries who cannot find work nearby are forced to endure long commutes to jobs elsewhere or to abandon their houses. The long waiting lists for housing, the limited choice of location and the dormitory nature of many state-subsidised housing environments create conditions that trap people in certain locations at the lowest end of the housing market.

Some beneficiaries have resorted to selling their houses, in many instances to non-South Africans who would otherwise be denied access to this form of housing. This represents a rational attempt to realise the asset value of the house. But these sales take place in defiance of express prohibitions against the right to sell and often reap less than the cost of construction.

The Housing Ministry has reacted to accusations that foreigners are occupying RDP houses illegally by suggesting that there is a need to audit subsidised housing and to take action against beneficiaries who have rented or sold their units. This criminalises people who are using their housing to increase their incomes through subletting or have been forced to move in search of jobs.

People sell their houses because in itself, the mere delivery of shelter does not reduce poverty. For housing to play a meaningful role in reducing poverty a different set of considerations is necessary: good location, access to social and infrastructural amenities and proximity to public transport routes, employment opportunities, schools and health facilities. The housing that is delivered needs to be usable as a social and financial asset. This means that planning regulations must permit the use of housing – within guidelines that protect quality of life – for income generation through subletting and home business.

The government has not been insensitive to criticisms levelled at RDP housing. One response has been to emphasise social housing. This is subsidised rental housing, generally located in the inner city, with demonstrable urban regeneration benefits. But again there are restrictive conditions of access: South African residency and monthly earnings of less than R7 500[5]. Beneficiaries need a steady income, a condition that many poor urban dwellers – South African or otherwise – cannot meet.

The response to these developments is often downward raiding, where people with higher incomes buy out the low-income beneficiaries and occupy units for which they would not qualify in terms of the income limits in the subsidy formula. Even though social housing is ostensibly a housing solution for the poor, it is primarily occupied by middle-income earners. A visitor to Johannesburg's social housing complexes is likely to see DStv aerials on the roofs and Mercedes-Benzes in the parking lots.

In a desperate attempt to address the housing needs of very poor urban residents, there have been some attempts by the state to provide emergency, transitional or communal housing. These are complexes that consist of a number of rooms with shared ablutions and cooking facilities. Yet again, the conditions of access are extremely restrictive.

People can access emergency housing if they are evicted, but an eviction process is often coupled with a round-up of 'illegal

THE MERE DELIVERY OF SHELTER DOES NOT REDUCE POVERTY.

INNER-CITY APARTMENT BLOCKS
OFTEN OPERATE AS VERTICAL GHETTOS.

aliens' by the Department of Home Affairs. More often than not, foreign-born residents are de-facto excluded from this housing. Rentals of R150 per bed a month are affordable. Entry to the building is tightly controlled, with tenants having to provide fingerprints or 'biometric identification' to gain access. Once they are inside, rules oblige residents to participate in cleaning and maintenance.

This housing acknowledges that many people cannot actually afford a self-contained unit: all they can afford is a room. It also acknowledges that many people in cities require only temporary accommodation. The few hundred beds provided by the City of Johannesburg do not begin to address the needs of the 55 000 new households which require accommodation. One-quarter of these households are considered migrant.

POPULAR RESPONSES

In the absence of appropriate housing provision by the state, the poor have taken on the task of housing themselves in a variety of creative ways including shacks, backyard accommodation and inner city rooms.

Rapidly erected shacks dominate this landscape. In Johannesburg 190 000 households live in shacks in about 180 informal settlements.[6] In theory almost anyone can occupy a shack. Shack settlements are often the key reception points for most new migrants to the cities, particularly foreign-born residents. Access to a shack settlement is heavily contingent on membership of a social network. This could be a local network or a network of people who come from the same country and who are all living in the same circumstances. Access may be tenuous, and as heavily dependent on systems of patronage as formal housing. Shack settlements often become physically and socially impenetrable to outsiders, ghettos of sorts.

Shack settlements offer poor quality housing, are particularly vulnerable to fire and have inadequate access to services. Their location in the city is variable. Sometimes shack settlements can be relatively well located on strategic bits of leftover land but shack settlements are often sited in flood zones or on geo-technically unstable land.

The persistent presence of shack settlements is a visible manifestation of failed state delivery. The state has set itself an ambitious target to eradicate shacks by 2014. This deadline is inspired by the Millennium Development Goals (MDG), which aim to improve the lives of slum-dwellers by 2014. But when the framers of the MDG said 'eradicate slums by 2014', they didn't have bulldozers and forced removals in mind.[7] The intention was that government should progressively improve shack settlements. The state has, at the very least, been ambiguous about shack settlements and, at worst, has misrepresented the MDG terminology.

In contrast, the City of Johannesburg is taking the MDG at its word and has very recently developed a policy to upgrade the city's informal settlements, in clear defiance of national policy rhetoric. It is too early to tell how Johannesburg's programme will unfold.

Another form of private delivery is backyard rooms. In Johannesburg an estimated 90 000 households live in backyard rooms. Conditions of access depend on some connection to the person living in the main house. The housing products are of

THE PERSISTENT PRESENCE OF SHACK SETTLEMENTS IS A VISIBLE MANIFESTATION OF FAILED STATE DELIVERY.

variable quality, in variable locations, but rents are affordable, starting at R150 a month. The letting of backyard rooms also allows the person occupying the main dwelling to use his/ her house as an income-producing asset.

The state views backyard rooms as inadequate, as part of the backlog, and as a drain on municipal infrastructure. But there is slow and grudging recognition from national government that maybe something interesting is happening in the backyard market. As yet, there are no formal attempts to address backyards and no regulations to manage the number of rooms per backyard, or the quality of the dwelling. It is a fundamental policy gap.

The third form of private delivery is inner-city rooms. Conditions of access depend mainly on whether the tenant can afford the rent. Some landlords specifically exclude 'foreigners', but there are social networks that may facilitate entry. Inner-city apartment blocks often operate as vertical ghettos. In Hillbrow certain buildings are known as 'Nigerian buildings', or 'Somalian buildings', or 'Ethiopian buildings'.

The location is excellent because it is in the city centre, within historically well-serviced residential areas. Rents vary, but if they prove unaffordable the tenant can advertise for a flatmate. In Hillbrow there is a wall where people advertise for sub-tenants to share rooms. The person responding to the advert will be a total stranger, which means that social conditions within the flat are likely to be tense.

The state's response to inner city sub-tenancy is opaque. There are building by-laws which facilitate evictions. If the state deems a particular building to be unfit there are mechanisms to prosecute the owner, and when the owner has absconded, to evict the tenants. In areas like Hillbrow,[8] the state operates in ambivalent ways: sporadic law enforcement and eviction, small amounts of state housing delivery, and a less active approach of waiting for the property market to make decisions. And significantly, the market has begun to move: there is rampant gentrification in Hillbrow. In response Hillbrow's developers, owners, and landlords are effecting a variety of quasi-legal mechanisms to secure their space and encourage further gentrification, and by extension, to increase rents.

An extraordinary range of living conditions exist. There are rooms in buildings where the electricity has been cut, rendering the sewer pumps inoperative, and where floods of raw sewerage are a regular occurrence. In an 'occupied'/ 'hijacked' building called San Jose there is a shebeen on one of the upper floors. In The Ridge, a run-down hotel, four Congolese men, one of whom manifests the symptoms of full-blown Aids, share a room and pay R150 per month per person. On the other hand there are newly renovated buildings that offer flats at R2 000 a month. One of these buildings is secured by a little gun turret from which an armed guard surveys the street. The guard has been known to remove street children from the pavement.

Maintenance of the public environment in these dense inner-city environments has deteriorated through a combination of neglect, overuse and deliberate withdrawal by the municipality in the face of unpaid municipal bills. The city will cut off the electricity in a building in the hope of compelling landlords to resume payment. Some landlords have reacted by installing their own generators, in effect privatising a collective municipal good.

AN EXTRAORDINARY RANGE
OF LIVING CONDITIONS EXIST.

These postmodern methods of delivering municipal services raise important questions about the ability of the state to retain control over systems that can easily fall into the hands of local private Mafiosi.

The informality that currently prevails in places like Hillbrow may not be appropriate. The level of technological sophistication within the average Hillbrow building – lifts, sewer pumps, complex water reticulation systems – are dependent on old-fashioned modernist notions of order and methods of management.

A NEW APPROACH

By occupying space illegally, informally or in other unregulated ways, the urban poor have succeeded in gaining a foothold in places that would otherwise be denied them. It is precisely in the space created by the absence of enforcement, by institutional flux and by ambivalence that the poor have managed to access the city. This is not to valorise informality. Informal housing strategies often result in inadequate living conditions and impenetrable ghetto-like enclaves, creating a problem both for the urban poor and the state, which seeks to fulfil their needs. These conditions result, over time, in the deterioration of the urban stage on which the poor themselves are reliant for their livelihoods.[9]

On the one hand it is necessary for the state to support the many creative responses that private individuals have devised to address their housing needs. At the same time, however, the state must curtail those private actions which undermine the urban collective on which we all depend: accessible public spaces and reliable municipal services.

THE URBAN POOR HAVE SUCCEEDED IN GAINING A FOOTHOLD IN PLACES THAT WOULD OTHERWISE BE DENIED THEM.

This suggests that the state needs to see cities – and housing – in a new way. This new approach should take cognisance of the many informal practices[10] that have emerged, and attempt to engage with these processes by providing some form of recognition – affording citizens' rights to 'foreigners', providing rudimentary forms of tenure to informal settlements, and actively upgrading the environments in which the poor regularly find themselves.

A new approach will require, at the very least, three initiatives. Firstly, the state needs to inititate a large-scale, national upgrading programme for informal settlements. This can deliver improved shelter in reasonable locations at the scale required to house the poor. Secondly, backyard shacks need to be recognised as an organic initiative to transform housing into income-producing assets, rather than dismissed as a social blight. Thirdly, there needs to be a dramatic increase in the delivery of well managed inner-city rooms.

Failure to do so will mean that the poor, both local and foreign-born, continue to live in vulnerable, precarious and dangerously combustible conditions. If the state does not respond in new ways, then competition for very scarce and increasingly degraded resources will intensify and ultimately threaten the lives not only of 'foreigners' but also of local poor people.

TWO NEWSPAPERS, TWO NATIONS?

THE MEDIA AND THE XENOPHOBIC VIOLENCE

ANTON HARBER

What is it we want from our media at a time of ugly anti-social violence? Brutal honesty, which would show that many of our compatriots are proud xenophobes? Caution and sensitivity, which would favour careful language and a choice of pictures to capture the hate which gripped our streets without offending or falling into tastelessness? Determined optimism, which would prioritise coverage of the few who show compassion above the many who show hatred? Or cold analysis, which would have us move quickly to probe the causes and effects?

These are questions I asked while taking a close look at the coverage of the first few days of the violence in May in two leading Johannesburg newspapers: the *Daily Sun* and *The Star*.

The *Daily Sun* is a mass market tabloid which has grown in the last few years to become the country's biggest daily by far, selling over 500 000 copies nationally, mostly to a working class readership. In its flamboyant way, the most noticeable aspect of this paper's coverage of the initial week of violence in May 2008 was its frequent and consistent use of the word 'aliens' to describe non-South Africans. The violence was flagged repeatedly in headlines as a 'war on aliens' ('It's war on aliens – 20 bust for attacks', 13 May; 'War against aliens: Thousands forced to flee Alex', 14 May).

In the tabloid tradition, 'aliens' usually refers to little green visitors from outer space, but the *Daily Sun* was referring to black visitors from much closer to home. The word has the same effect: emphasising foreigners as outsiders, different and strange, not part of us, even threatening. To describe the violence as 'war' implies a formal exercise in defending the country against this invasion, and invokes such dramatic phrases as 'war on terror'.[1]

It is striking that the *Daily Sun*, in contrast with most other media, downplayed the violence. On the first Monday after the violence broke out in Alexandra, the *Daily Sun* had no coverage, though this was probably due to early Sunday deadlines. On day two, it had only a short inside story. The first time the story appeared on its front page was on Wednesday, three days after the violence broke out and when it had dominated national headlines for 48 hours. The angle it took was of a 'homeboy' mistaken for an 'alien'. It would be hard to think of two phrases which more clearly distinguish between local and foreign. The story kicked off with a stark warning, in bold type, to its (local) readers: 'Be very careful ... don't look or act like a foreigner.' If there was ever a call to South Africans to keep their distance from foreigners, this was it.

IT WAS NOTICEABLY NOT OFFERING EVEN A HINT OF CRITICISM OF THE VIOLENCE AND BLOODSHED.

Over the next few days, the *Daily Sun* paid some attention to the victims of the violence, and much focus on South Africans who were in danger of becoming victims. 'But cops say one of the victims was South African' appeared high up in its very first story. And: 'So far four aliens have died. And now South Africans are victims too – mainly Shangaans and Vendas.'

The paper showed its colours most starkly on day four, the Thursday, with a front-page editorial purporting to tell 'the Truth' about 'aliens'.

'There is much wailing about the debt we owe foreigners, the lessons we learnt from our own struggle, the dignity of all Africans, the evils of xenophobia – the big word for hatred of foreigners. There are calls for indabas and workshops on the subject. WHAT NONSENSE,' the *Daily Sun* said with its characteristic disdain for long words and the people who use them. Talking serves little point, it was saying, and it was noticeably not offering even a hint of criticism of the violence and bloodshed.

The *Daily Sun* then suggested the 'real' reasons for what was going on. Its explanation started quite routinely, pointing to high unemployment, corruption in housing allocations and government's lack of policy on foreigners. It pointed fingers of blame at the authorities, but, given an absence of condemnation of the killings and lootings, it also appeared to be suggesting that South Africans had cause to hate foreigners.

But then fairly low down in its story came the kicker: 'Many of us live in fear of foreign gangsters and conmen. Much terror has been caused by gangs of armed Zimbabweans, Mozambicans and others.' That was followed by a generous concession: 'Not every foreigner is a gangster, of course – but too many are.'

WHAT IS IT WE WANT FROM OUR MEDIA AT
A TIME OF UGLY ANTI-SOCIAL VIOLENCE?

Foreigners were not just alien, they were criminal aliens, in the *Daily Sun's* pages. The one consensus we seem to have in our society is that criminals are fair game. 'Shoot the bastards,' the Deputy Minister of Safety and Security recently said.[2] Label people criminals and you are setting them up for attack.

The *Daily Sun* could not criticise the president for being slow to speak out, as it was even slower. It did not condemn the violence until a full two weeks later in a column by the editor. Interestingly, after the editor's condemnation of the violence, the *Daily Sun* appeared to stop using the word 'aliens', signalling a deliberate shift in its coverage.

But to point to the *Daily Sun's* willingness to pander to xenophobic sentiments is to see only half the picture and it is a common failing among South African media analysts to take a narrow view of the role of this unusual newspaper. Below the 'Aliens: The Truth' headline was a picture of two bodies and a burning bakkie. It was described as a civilian attack on suspected criminals, with no mention of nationality. And in fact on the previous day, the xenophobia story was tucked away on page 4, and more prominence was given to the page 5 lead, 'Residents on the rampage' over a lack of basic services. In that week, the paper had no fewer than three prominent stories of citizens turning into vigilantes to deal with alleged criminals.

None of these stories appeared in any other media that I could find. The *Daily Sun* covers township life like no-one else, telling us about a range of violent protests, and treated the xenophobic attacks as just one manifestation of people's anger and frustration.

This points to the wider role that the *Daily Sun* is playing. It is covering people and events not found in any other media and

in doing so is giving an identity and public space to citizens who don't otherwise have it. It is articulating a frustration and anger which, distasteful as it may often be, is real and substantial, and is thus providing a warning signal of a number of developments that are covered in other media only when they explode into crises.

I randomly take today's *Daily Sun* as I write this (10 June 2008) and find it has a horrifying picture of a burnt man, a suspected criminal killed brutally by his neighbours. It is not reported nor photographed anywhere else that I can find. If you want evidence that ordinary citizens are responding in a particular way to anger around crime, it is there. You have to cut through the *Daily Sun's* gung-ho and triumphant reporting of vigilantism, but the other news media will likely only cover it when it bursts out of the townships or becomes a national crisis in some other visible way.

Daily Sun founder and publisher, Deon du Plessis, wrote a defence of his paper's treatment of foreigners a few weeks later in the *Mail & Guardian*. 'Batting for the home team' is how he characterised his attitude, likening the paper's attitude to fans supporting their local sports team. 'It may not be a very worldly view,' he said, but it served the paper's audience, 'the Guy in the Blue Overall'. This guy did not have the luxury of those in 'august circles' who could take worldly views of foreigners and who talked of 'one brotherhood'. (And 'sisterhood!', Du Plessis added, with the exclamation point to denote how surprised his guy would be at such a phrase.)

This blue-overalled guy is 'not so sure about that' brotherhood stuff, he said. He has a struggle to survive and doesn't have the luxury to share what he has won so far. Faced with a government that is failing him, battling daily with 'crass and often useless

BUT THE OTHER NEWS MEDIA WILL LIKELY ONLY COVER IT WHEN IT BURSTS OUT OF THE TOWNSHIPS OR BECOMES A NATIONAL CRISIS IN SOME OTHER VISIBLE WAY.

officialdom', this guy knows just one comforting thing: 'The nation's biggest daily is right there, batting for him every day.'

Batting for him means, in Du Plessis' mind, reflecting the fact that he is full of anger and resentment towards the many foreigners he sees around him.

* * *

Two things are immediately apparent in *The Star*'s coverage. *The Star* is the country's second-biggest daily, but with sales of about 160 000 falls far behind its tabloid rival. It is the flagship of the Independent Group of newspapers and is pitched at Johannesburg middle-class suburban households. From the outset of the violence, the paper was doing substantial first-hand reporting, with a team of reporters and photographers on the ground and much of the paper devoted to the story. Its coverage was fuller than any of the other Johannesburg dailies, its pictures used large and dramatically, dominating the front pages. Its focus was almost entirely on the victims. Its choice of gruesome pictures, its screaming headlines, its stories told the tales of the targets of violence.

For example, on day one of the coverage, Monday 12 May, *The Star* featured two huge and horrifying colour pictures of bloodied victims under the bold headline: 'Faces of xenophobic hate: Victims tell of night of terror ...' The newspaper was deliberate in humanising these individuals, with close-ups of their faces, and the core of the story was the victims giving their account of what had happened. On the Thursday, it built a front page around a picture of school students tormenting refugees through the

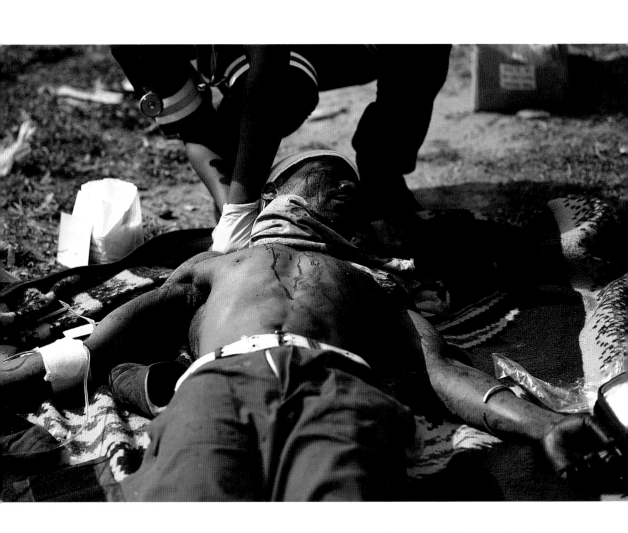

THE DISTANCE BETWEEN *THE STAR* REPORTERS
AND THE PERPETRATORS WAS PALPABLE.

fence of a police station. 'Kids learn the lesson of hate' was the headline. Once again the pictures and quotes told the story from the victims' viewpoint.

The following week, it was one of two newspapers which went to the trouble of identifying and telling the story of the man burnt alive before the cameras, which had provided the most horrific image of the violence, one flashed across the world. It took some work to uncover this story, but *The Star* made a point of individualising him by finding his friends and family and telling us bits and pieces of his life.

The perpetrators, on the other hand, were a 'mob' (a word used over and over again in *The Star*) and were described with words like 'bloodlust' and 'gang'. The distance between the *Star* reporters and the perpetrators was palpable: '*They* came in the night carrying iron bars … *They* came hunting foreigners …'

On its pages, in contrast to the *Daily Sun*, it was the attackers who were largely faceless and anonymous. *The Star* was quick to condemn the violence, but you would have had to search hard in its pages to get a clear understanding of who the attackers were and what drove them. There was an isolated quote here or there to give some indication, but little of substance.

By the second week, the story of violence was supplanted by the humanitarian crisis, and *The Star* gave over the front pages to calls for help and assistance, and even set up its own fund. Pictures of refugee children were used to evoke sympathy and the paper's civic role displaced the hard news. 'Please help this little girl' was the front page headline for the launch of what it called 'a campaign to show the real heart of South Africa'. And the next day it was 'Love vs hate: The nation fights back', featuring a girls' school protesting against the violence and donating for peace. It was feel-good stuff as it asserted an image of South Africans as loving and caring, in contrast to the brutal images which went around the world and dominated *The Star's* own front page.

A few weeks later, *The Star* published a special supplement analysing the causes of the violence and trying to point the way ahead. The title, 'Never Again', evoked the message of Nelson Mandela's landmark inauguration speech of 1994. The paper also organised a public forum to discuss the implications of the outbreak of violence. There was a special effort to give depth to the coverage and ask questions which pushed beyond daily reporting towards identifying solutions. The voices used for this were notably those of scholars, analysts and politicians. Not a blue overall was in sight.

* * *

So we had contrasting treatments of the same story: one paper focused on South Africans as victims, and came close to legitimising attacks on foreigners, giving its front page over to telling why South Africans had reason to hate foreigners; the other focused on foreigners as victims, and launched a sympathy campaign, giving its front page over to appeals for demonstrations of caring and organising public discussions and campaigns.

It is easy to say which of these newspaper treatments would have made South Africans feel better about themselves: *The Star* held out hope that those who responded to humanitarian needs won out over those who participated in the violence or

ONE CAN ONLY START TO SEE SOUTH AFRICA BY READING BOTH PAPERS, WITH TREPIDATION.

stood aside as it happened. It is tougher to say which newspaper offered the more accurate depiction of our society. Rather, they offered the perspectives of the suburban white collar and the township blue overall respectively, filtered through journalists playing to those particular audiences.

This takes us back to the question of what we expected of our newspapers in this situation. If it was foremost to tell us what was happening day-to-day at the height of the conflict, *The Star* did well. If it was to evoke sympathy and an outpouring of public healing, *The Star* did well again. If it was to express the darkest sentiments of the angry and the powerless, you would have to give credit to the *Daily Sun*. For forewarning that such sentiments are lurking in the hearts of many South Africans and are bursting out in small ways all the time, the *Daily Sun* again.

If we expected our papers to probe the events and find out what lay behind them, what drives South Africans to act with such callous brutality, *The Star* gave us a special supplement of learned commentary and an august panel discussion, and the *Daily Sun* gave us its version of what 'the Guy in the Blue Overall' was saying.

Taken together, we have a stark contrast in treatment and perspectives, both partial, both incomplete, each serving and playing to different audiences. There is no overlap in readership between the two. If a good newspaper is a nation talking to itself, as Arthur Miller once said, then we have here two nations talking to themselves. The conclusion has to be that one can only start to see South Africa by reading both papers, with trepidation.

BEYOND CITIZENSHIP

HUMAN RIGHTS AND DEMOCRACY

CATHI ALBERTYN

For many South Africans the recent xenophobic violence betrayed fundamental values of community, inclusion, participation and *ubuntu* and confirmed just how far we are from the democratic society imagined by those who wrote the new Constitution in the early 1990s.

That Constitution created a common and inclusive citizenship, finally granting all South Africans the basic right of citizenship – the right to vote for a government of one's choice. However, the 1993 (interim) Constitution contemplated more than political freedom. It imagined an inclusive and participatory democracy, a new society based on human rights and democratic values. In the words of the late Constitutional Court Justice, Ismail Mahomed, this was no ordinary constitution seeking merely 'to formalise, in a legal instrument, a historical consensus of values and aspirations, evolved incrementally from a stable and unbroken past to accommodate the needs of the future'. On the contrary, it 'represent[ed] a decisive break from ... the past ... and [expressed a] commitment to a democratic, universalist, caring and aspirationally egalitarian ethos'.[1] The court, and many lawyers, judges and human rights activists came to describe this Constitution – and its 1996 successor – as a transformative document which guides South Africa as it seeks to '[h]eal the divisions of the past and establish a society based on democratic values, social justice and fundamental rights'.[2]

The commitment to transformation that lies at the heart of the new constitutional order is guided by the democratic values of human dignity, the achievement of equality, and freedom. It is also guided by the spirit of *ubuntu* – expressed by the Constitutional Court as

> describing the significance of group solidarity on survival issues so central to the survival of communities. While it envelops the key values of group solidarity, compassion, respect, human dignity, conformity to basic norms and collective unity, in its fundamental sense it denotes humanity and morality. Its spirit emphasises respect for human dignity, marking a shift from confrontation to conciliation.[3]

The constitutional aspiration of a transformed society envisages engaged compassionate citizens within an open, transparent and accountable state. Its reach extends beyond a narrow idea of a community of citizens to a broadly caring society, inclusive of all who live here. This is apparent in the constitutional text and in

XENOPHOBIC VIOLENCE BETRAYED FUNDAMENTAL VALUES
OF COMMUNITY, INCLUSION, PARTICIPATION AND UBUNTU.

its interpretation. In all but a handful of rights enumerated in the Bill of Rights, the subject of the right is 'everyone'. The fact that 'everyone' extends beyond citizens is confirmed by the fact that 'citizens' are expressly granted only two sets of rights: political rights, as in rights to vote, form political parties and stand for political office, and the right of choice in trade, occupation and profession. All other rights – including rights to dignity, equality, life, freedom and security of the person and a range of socio-economic rights, such as access to water, social assistance, housing, education and health care – are given to 'everyone'. 'Everyone' thus includes those who are not citizens.

Several judgments of the Constitutional Court have addressed the place of those who are not South African citizens in our constitutional democracy. For example, the powerful equality clause that guarantees freedom from unfair discrimination on a range of grounds does not list citizenship or nationality as a prohibited basis for discrimination. When asked to consider adding citizenship to the list of prohibited grounds, the court had little problem in doing so. In *Larbi-Odam v MEC for Education (North West Province)*,[4] a case concerning the right of permanent residents to be granted permanent teaching posts, the court concluded that unjust treatment based on nationality has the potential to impair the fundamental dignity of persons as human beings: as a minority, foreign citizens lack political power and are vulnerable to having their interests overlooked and being seen as less worthy than South Africans.[5] This case established 'citizenship' or 'nationality' as a prohibited ground of discrimination in South Africa and confirmed foreign nationals as part of the community of people protected by the Constitution.

THE COURT SPOKE ABOUT THE COLLECTIVE RESPONSIBILITY THAT WE, AS A COMMUNITY, HAVE TO THOSE WHO ARE POOR AND DESTITUTE.

Foreign nationals living in South Africa are, of course, a diverse group not only in terms of nationality, language, religion, socio-economic status and so forth, but also in their different positions as permanent or temporary residents, with or without permission to be present in South Africa. They include many groups. Permanent residents have permission to live and work here and apply for citizenship after five years. Temporary visitors may come to South Africa for trade, work, vacation or study. Refugees from conflict and persecution enjoy rights to live and work under the Refugees Act once their refugee status is recognised, while asylum-seekers hope to secure such status. Unless lawfully present under one or other category, foreign nationals are vulnerable to arrest and deportation.

The courts have dealt with several cases relating to the violation of the rights of permanent residents and refugees. *Larbi-Odam*, mentioned above, saw foreign teachers challenge the preferential treatment granted South African teachers in North West Province, which resulted in permanent residents not being able to obtain permanent teaching posts, and even losing their jobs if citizens applied for their post. In finding this to constitute unfair discrimination, the court rejected the stereotypes and prejudicial assumptions that informed this policy. For example, it rejected the idea that it was the sole duty of government to reduce employment amongst South Africans. In the context of the state's duty to provide education, the court found that there should be no distinction in the treatment of educators who are permanent residents and those who are citizens. There was thus no justification for the preference of permanent residents over citizens in seeking to reduce unemployment.[6] The court also noted the adverse impact of a lack of job tenure on people's ability to live secure lives and exercise personal life choices in pursuit of their well-being and that of their families.[7]

The recognition of the dignity of all, citizens and foreign nationals alike, was reiterated by the Supreme Court of Appeal in 2004:

> Human dignity has no nationality. It is inherent in all people – citizens and non-citizens alike – simply because they are human. And while that person happens to be in this country – for whatever reason – it must be respected, and is protected, by [the right to dignity in] ... the Bill of Rights.[8]

Perhaps the most significant judgment on the rights of foreign nationals is *Khosa v Minister of Social Development*.[9] In this case, a community of destitute permanent residents, originally from Mozambique, argued that making access to social grants dependent on citizenship was unfair discrimination and a violation of their right of access to social security under the Constitution. The court agreed. In doing so, it rejected the argument that only citizens had a legitimate claim to social security or that the exclusion of permanent residents was justified as they could apply for citizenship after only five years. It also found, on the evidence, that the additional expenditure required to extend social grants to permanent residents would not place an intolerable financial burden on the state, and did not justify the exclusion of permanent residents from the grants.

What is particularly important about this judgment is the manner in which it envisages a compassionate community that extends beyond citizens to embrace those who are in need and

HUMAN DIGNITY HAS NO NATIONALITY.

WE ARE RESPONSIBLE FOR THE WELL-BEING OF OTHERS.

have been marginalised in our society. Thus the court spoke about the collective responsibility that we, as a community, have to those who are poor and destitute:

> Sharing responsibility for the problems and consequences of poverty equally as a community represents the extent to which wealthier members of the community view the minimal well-being of the poor as connected with their personal well-being and the well-being of the community as a whole.

Khosa was a courageous and principled decision that was not universally welcomed, especially in its willingness to override the policy and financial arguments of the state. Yet its portrayal of the South African community as a caring and compassionate one resonates with the principle of *ubuntu* and the idea that we are responsible for the well-being of others. The court's conception of a state and society that actively care for those in need is the high-water mark of constitutional jurisprudence on the treatment of foreign nationals living in South Africa, capturing the constitutional vision of an inclusive society based on dignity, equality and freedom. It is a vision that signifies the best that we can be.

Disappointingly, a later case on the rights of refugees falls short of these aspirations. In *Union of Refugee Women v Director of the Private Security Industry Regulatory Authority,*[10] refugees working as car guards and menial security workers challenged legal provisions that made it particularly difficult to register as security workers, unless a citizen or permanent resident. This case began to reveal the faultlines in the court's treatment of foreign nationals.

The Constitutional Court recognised refugees as a vulnerable group in our society and that their plight calls for compassion.[11] However, in a convenient sleight of hand, the majority of judges found that the legislative scheme was not an issue of unfair discrimination, but properly fell within a right limited to citizens – namely choice of occupation. Not only was the exclusion of refugees justified on this basis, but the court also found that the security of the public justified the requirement that foreign nationals, who were not permanent residents, should prove their trustworthiness as security workers.

In a principled dissenting judgment, Justices Yvonne Mokgoro, Kate O'Regan and Pius Langa disagreed. They noted that refugees are a particular class of foreign nationals who, once recognised, have a right to remain in the country indefinitely accordingly to the provisions of the Refugees Act. They are thus a vulnerable group, in a similar position to permanent residents, and discrimination against them has the potential to impair their dignity. In testing whether the discrimination in the law was unfair, the judges found as follows:

[The majority of the court] found that the purpose of [the law] was to ensure that security services providers are trustworthy. While the purpose is worthy, we cannot agree that giving effect to the purpose through section 23(1)(a) is legitimate as it appears to be based on an illegitimate silent premise. The premise may be that foreign nationals, including refugees, are as a group inherently less trustworthy than South Africans. In our view, such a premise is not supported by any evidence placed before the Court and would amount to unfair and damaging stereotyping of foreign nationals.

The justices went on to find that '[e]xcluding refugees from the right to work as private security providers simply because they are refugees will inevitably foster a climate of xenophobia which will be harmful to refugees and inconsistent with the overall vision of our Constitution'.[12] The impact of this is both social and material – stigmatising refugees as less worthy and denying them the ability to find work in an industry that is a significant source of employment for many refugees. This has 'a severe impact on the ability of refugees to earn a livelihood in South Africa'.[13]

It is interesting that the court falters in a case dealing with basic forms of employment, suggesting that it is in access to jobs and resources for the poor that the divisions between 'insider' (citizen or permanent resident) and 'outsider' (refugee, asylum seeker) are most keenly felt. It is left to a minority of three judges to perceive the dangers of this approach, and the manner in which social and material exclusion are so intertwined.

The contrasting judgments in this case are thus testimony to the precarious nature of the constitutional promise of a better society. The Constitution's vision of a democratic, universalist, caring and aspirationally egalitarian ethos is all too easily undermined – not only in the terrible xenophobic violence of May 2008, but also in the operation of our own prejudices and stereotypes. The faultlines run throughout our society. Overcoming those prejudices is as much about addressing the material issues of poverty and inequality as it is about interrogating the norms and values by which we all live. For those of us committed to social justice, that means working practically and intellectually to engage with the kind of society that the Constitution promotes and the ways in which we think it can be achieved.

WE ARE NOT ALL LIKE THAT

RACE, CLASS AND NATION AFTER APARTHEID

ANDILE MNGXITAMA

The SMSs came fast and furious. As furious as the fiery images we were subjected to by our television and our daily newspapers. The front pages were a festival of beastly pictures of the victims of the negrophobic bloodletting which gripped South Africa in the past weeks. I dreaded opening a newspaper for days – afraid of being confronted by yet another grisly product of the negrophobic xenophobic violence, which by the end of week three had claimed the lives of over 60 people and displaced about 100 000, according to some estimates. The mind spins out of the axis of the normal.

As Alexandra township burnt, I read text messages from my cappuccino-loving Tito Mboweni-fearing middle class friends. The messages were generally along these lines: 'I'm so embarrassed to be South African right now' or more engaging: 'I'm so tired of feeling angry about this and not being able to do something about it ...'. Email lists held similar messages of shame. At least Winnie Madikizela-Mandela went to Alexandra and told the terrified victims cramped at the police station: 'We are sorry, please forgive us. South Africans are not like this' before hopping back into her nice car and driving back to her life. Desmond Tutu followed with another 'Sorry, we are not like that'.

The leader of the narrow Zulu nationalist movement, Mangosuthu Buthelezi, went to the police station as well and cried for the cameras, at the same time as his followers from the hostel he had just addressed continued their war cry that they would kill all the 'foreigners', *Hambani*! Our president-in-waiting, Jacob Zuma, was told by an angry crowd: 'Go back to Mozambique with your Mozambicans.' Apparently his favourite solo *'Umshini wam'* was sung by the marauding gangs as they went about their murderous deeds. The killings, burning and looting continued. Something had definitely broken, the despised were telling their leaders in their faces that they must all go to hell.

The next day, an SMS announced the clarion call: 'Fight xenophobia! Donate food, clothes and money if possible.'

One of my friends had been working non-stop, even on weekends, to try do something to ease the hardships of the refugees now cramped in police stations and other camps. I asked my exhausted friend, but why don't you cook a big meal once in a while and send it down to our permanent refugee camps? She burst out laughing.

Truth is, the many squatter camps which host millions of South Africans are nothing but permanent refugee camps. The multitudes that are trapped in these squatter camps are the

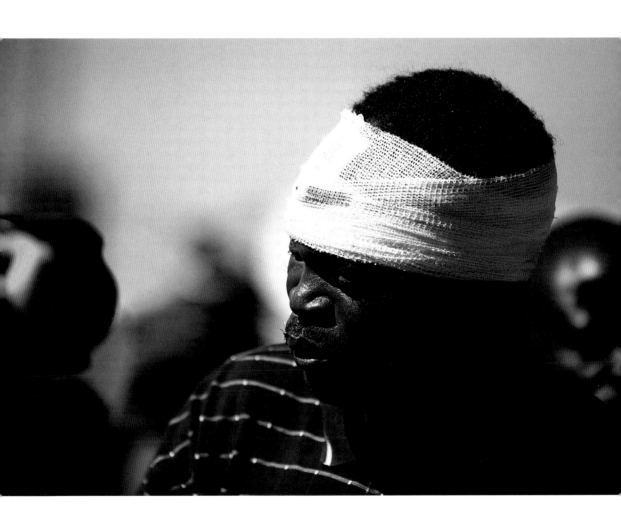

THE FRONT PAGES WERE A FESTIVAL OF BEASTLY PICTURES
OF THE VICTIMS OF THE NEGROPHOBIC BLOODLETTING.

THE KILLINGS, BURNING
AND LOOTING CONTINUED.
SOMETHING HAD DEFINITELY
BROKEN, THE DESPISED WERE
TELLING THEIR LEADERS
IN THEIR FACES THAT
THEY MUST ALL GO TO HELL.

excluded of our democracy. Their lives are punctuated daily by the violence of hunger, denigration, hopelessness and perpetual terror of what the state is going to do next. The state, led by black Africans, regularly sends out the message that black Africans are undesirables.

Week two: In slow motion the human rights industry, the government and social movements started to respond to the violence. Frantic meetings were called. White liberals mobilised assistance for the refugees, not entirely altruistically. Help is the most potent form of exercising power. The donor world opened its humanitarian wallets. For the first time in a long time I heard that money was not the problem. So besides the weekly meetings coordinated by our Chapter 9 institutions (the Human Rights Commission, the Commission on Gender Equality, the Office of the Public Protector, etc), the social movements called a march through Hillbrow.

The mayhem continued in other parts of Gauteng. The squatter camps continued to burn, the death toll rose. Three demands from both the chapter 9s and civil society became solidified: bring in the army, set up special courts to try the perpetrators and declare a moratorium on arrests and deportations of black Africans. Later a fourth call emerged: where is the president of the country?

The soldiers came in, the special court was prepared, but a moratorium on deporting the undesirables was proving tricky. The relevant minister issued a statement. Some people celebrated, but they hadn't read the small print. She said, 'Possible suggestions included issuing temporary residence permits ...' I think it is here where champagne corks were popped, but in the haste to celebrate we didn't hear her say '...so that everyone in the country would at least be recorded and fingerprinted, in the interests of security and stability'. Tell you what, if I'm black and from the African continent and have seen what the government of South Africa has done to us in the past 14 years I would run away with my fingerprints.

As it always happens, the psychology of violence operates on the basis of the weakest link. The *kwerekweres* are already marked out for harassment by state institutions. Now the poor citizenry are finishing off the job in a demented frenzy. Now we are calling on the same government to help quell the violence it has helped structure. We have a crisis on our hands; thinking is outlawed.

Those of us who express moral outrage at this barbarity are unified by one main consideration – we are not like them, the mad, backward, blood-thirsty barbarians who don't know that we are all Africans. They are stupid idiotic fools, *sies bayasinyanyisa*! I think about the hidden relief of Ivan's friends in Tolstoy's short masterpiece *The Death of Ivan Ilych*. At one point Tolstoy reports: 'In addition to speculations as to the possible changes and promotions which the news of his death gave rise to, the very fact of the death of one they had known so well made each of them rejoice that it was his friend rather than himself who had died.' In this case, we, the enlightened middle classes, are in some ways delighted that it was not us who burnt the *kwerekweres*. We wouldn't do something like that, would we now?

Tolstoy says it better: 'Fancy that: he is dead, I'm not.' They are evil barbarians, we are not. They would be condemned, we shall not. We condemn them.

THE PSYCHOLOGY OF VIOLENCE OPERATES ON THE BASIS OF THE WEAKEST LINK.

The Saturday morning of the march we gather at a park on the base of Hillbrow, the notorious and controversial seedy suburb long abandoned by God and whites. Colourful scarves, branded Crocs shoes, babies strapped on backs or in trendy prams, it's a happy multiracial march of the enlightened. We snake through Hillbrow, the dangerous suburb we can't be caught dead in. There are teary moments when a building full of hands waves at our courageous and righteous stand. We wave back, we whistle and clap hands, it's a cool sixties-like moment – 'one love!' – black and white together, it's a reassuring illusion. We are euphoric; the lapsed left of yesteryear has come out of the woodwork. The golf course can wait until later.

It's better to think of this outbreak of black violence as some atavistic unexplainable black lashing out at black. Some deep black thing still untamed by our white God and white education. A failed socialisation process. Civilisation has not yet touched the deep recesses of these barbarians. But at least we are not like them. To think of this violence as a consequence of the relatively comfortable lives we lead would be too much. But the creation of Sandton, that super-rich suburb, was made possible by the creation of the sprawling Alexandra, a *favela* right at its doorstep. Alexandra is the direct product of Sandton. This is a troubling formulation: it points an accusatory finger at the rich. And to be rich is to be white. It says: 'The violence you see is an outcome of the plunder of your forbears.' There are no white *kwerekweres* in our country.

The events of the last three weeks are not caused by xenophobia; 'negrophobia' is a more accurate term. Chinweizu describes negrophobia: 'The fear and dislike of blacks is a great disease. It has killed more blacks in the last five hundred years than all other diseases combined: more than malaria, more than epidemics and plagues of all sorts. In the coming years, it could kill far more than AIDS. It is a psychological disease, a disease of the mind, which harvests dead black bodies every day.' [1]

We hate the poor because they remind us that black is bad. We march and declare their barbarity because we want to assure our white counterparts and ourselves that we are human just like the whites, we are not like the barbarians killing each other mercilessly. We plead, 'There is nothing to fear from us.' We hate because this violence heightens our sense of the 'nervous condition'. We are afraid to be found out and maybe also to find out that our blackness has not been erased totally. The smug smile in the face of our enlightened white liberal friends and colleagues terrifies us because it says, 'You are cannibals!' So we march with our white friends, hand in hand, as guarantors of our common humanity. But we fall short. This bloody black skin. Go away, my black skin!

This negrophobic violence is not new; anyone who lives in a township or squatter camp knows that it is your brothers who will be slaughtering you for your cellphone when the sun goes down at night. Now this violence has been externalised to the *kwerekweres*; they are easy targets. Have we pointed to the real source of this evil? Has that source now been given a little melanin for beautification post-1994? To point to history and show that the current violence is not new and is a direct consequence of the wealth a few enjoy is to ask for accounting. No, let's not go there. So march on.

Some whites call in to radio talk shows, some even write a few letters to the newspapers with concern. If they are killing

HAVE WE POINTED TO THE REAL SOURCE OF THIS EVIL?

foreigners, soon they are going to say whites are foreigners too. We must fight xenophobia, it is not good, it can lead to civil war. Yes, once they finish the *kwerekweres*, in three months, there would still be no houses, no jobs or women. What do they do then? What can they do? Who knows?

But our white counterparts should sleep easy; the job of damaging the black mind has been thorough. Steve Biko says, '… the type of black man (sic) we have today has lost his manhood. Reduced to an obliging shell, he looks with awe at the white power structure and accepts what he regards as the "inevitable position". Deep inside his anger mounts at the accumulating insult, but he vents it in the wrong direction – on his fellow men in the township, on the property of black people.'[2]

The creation of the beastly black is directly linked to the development of the South African socio-economic system. When the colonialist and the missionaries found us idle and happy in our fat-smeared bodies, they gave us the fear of hell, covered our bodies in Western clothes, poisoned our minds with their superiority and at gunpoint saved us from our idleness and forced us into the civilising rigours of labour. For those who still refused to work they took their land and forced them to pay all sorts of crazy taxes. We were trapped. Didn't the rogue murderous blood-thirsty civiliser Cecil John Rhodes, in a moment of arrogant honesty, tell us point-blank that: 'Every black man cannot have three acres and a cow or four morgen and a commonage right. We have to face the question and it must be brought home to them [blacks] that in the future nine-tenths of them will have to spend their lives in daily labour.'[3]

We were lied to. Karl Marx was wrong to think that one has to go through the barbarity of capitalism to reach the end

WE MUST FIGHT XENOPHOBIA, IT IS NOT GOOD, IT CAN LEAD TO CIVIL WAR.

of the cruel and stultifying division of labour. The bearded one was articulate about his communist nirvana: 'To do one thing today and another tomorrow, to hunt in the morning, fish in the afternoon, rear cattle in the evening ... without ever becoming hunter, fisherman, shepherd, or critic.'[4] We were there before all of this white madness, forcing men to abandon their families to dig for gold. Our deeply contemplative lives, exemplified by the Khoisan, were condemned. But actually they were all jealous of our state of advanced existence. The best of their thinkers were depicting such great liberation from nature and want as signifying progress of historical proportion. Epoch-making stuff.

But things have changed; we now want to work. We are killing each other for the crumbs Rhodes spat out of his rotten mouth. We want jobs! We want to be in daily labour. To eat one must work. We are trapped in the animal level of existence, we want food and we are going to slaughter each other for it. To live we must kill each other. We are cannibals.

We fail to ask a simple question: 'How come we are so hungry when food is not the problem?' How come no one is seeing that the rapid rise of food prices has removed all bonds of human co-existence from the famished bodies of the excluded? How come no one sees lack of food as the trigger to the massive slaughter we have witnessed in the past few weeks? In isiXhosa we say *indlala inamnyala*. A rough translation of this is: 'If we misbehave, don't blame us, blame our stomachs.'

The shame which has moved the middle classes to feign concern has little to do with concern for the victims or for the wellbeing of fellow human beings. If we did care we would long

ago have seen the everyday structural violence in which the majority of poor blacks are trapped. We would long ago have asked the question, why so much poverty in the midst of so much plenty? Instead we focused on stuffing our pockets and mouths. In fact we hate the poor, we hate them because they remind us so powerfully where we could end up and where we come from.

When our president eventually decided to address the nation, he appeared in the middle of our TV screens and kept quiet. He was a little black dot. He just sat there motionless making strange noises at best but saying nothing to help us either understand the causes of violence or the measures our beloved democratic country was taking to fight the root causes. For 15 minutes, our intellectual president simply stared at us. We stared back. Mutual misrecognition.

Those who have tried to explain the violence have only shown parts of the whole. For most, history has been forgotten, and the key source, ill-begotten wealth, shielded from view. The fact that ours is a neo-apartheid state managed now by yesterday's anti-apartheid revolutionaries is also concealed.

Some have called for the decolonisation of the mind, others have called for a focus on the economics of neo-liberalism. Frantz Fanon warned against this atomisation of the mind and socio-economic and political realities. Let it be said again, it is true the problem is both psychological and a matter of livelihoods. Fanon advised: '... It is apparent to me that the effective disalienation of the black man entails an immediate recognition of the social and economic realities. If there is an inferiority complex, it is the outcome of a double process:

WE HATE THE POOR, WE HATE THEM BECAUSE THEY REMIND US SO POWERFULLY WHERE WE COULD END UP AND WHERE WE COME FROM.

- Primarily, economic;
- Subsequently, the internalisation – or, better, the epidermalisation of this inferiority.'[5]

Fanon later on advises that the battle against alienation of the black must be fought on both levels (economic and psychological), because 'any unilateral liberation is incomplete, and the gravest mistake would be to believe in their automatic interdependence'. He also says: 'There will be an authentic disalienation only to the degree to which things, in the most materialistic meaning of the world, will have been restored to their proper places.'[6] Here we see that without liberation there can be no salvation.

The question remains, what does it mean to be free, for blacks? At the same time we must ask, what would it take to restore things to their proper places? Is the current black-on-black cannibalism a spiral to the bottom of existence where we blacks rightfully belong or is it a dress rehearsal for the end of the world? Biko says: 'Ground for a revolution is always fertile in the presence of absolute destitution. At some stage one can foresee a situation where black people will feel they have nothing to live for and will shout at their God, "Thy will be done".' [7] Are we hearing a disfigured moan which could find its range and turn into a shout?

BRUTAL INHERITANCES

ECHOES, NEGROPHOBIA AND MASCULINIST VIOLENCE

PUMLA DINEO GQOLA

It's the agents of our imagination which really shape who we are.

Chris Abani, Arusha, Tanzania

Truth is unreliable, so we use narratives to make sense of ourselves, many times reliant on stereotypes and historical rumours.

Jennifer Musangi, Johannesburg, South Africa

I returned to a recording of Chris Abani's 2007 TED[1] talk immediately after attending a workshop at which various Kenyan intellectuals made sense of the frightening post-election violence in that country. Musangi, to whom I had listened earlier, seemed to be in conversation with Abani. Abani spoke about the often dangerous ways in which language can be inflected to brutalise or to achieve its inverse and open up possibilities, adding that 'language can only be understood in the context of story'. Musangi's attention was on the many ways in which Kenyan stories of ethnicity code tensions that cannot be easily explained. Here, past wrongs are recalled, imagined and reconfigured to tell a story that has relevance in the present.

This is not where the 'conversation' between Musangi and Abani ends, however. Over the next few days, as I try to produce this essay, I find myself returning to their words, and turning to their thoughts repeatedly. The outbreak of what the media and various South African publics have dubbed xenophobia has underscored the danger of narratives of hate. Insofar as I remain deeply unsatisfied by the vast majority of explanations offered by South African analysts and intellectuals, as during other times of great difficulty, I turn towards the words of writers whose words I deeply value. In this essay, this is the route I choose to make sense of what the 'xenophobic' attacks culminating in May 2008 meant. Abani's and Musangi's words are particularly useful because in the specific addresses I reference, they too attempt to make sense of the links between language and 'unexpected' violence.

Abani recalls a joke he heard often as a child about Tom, Dick and, finally, Harry, the brunt of the humour. Harry's inexplicable behaviour ('untrustworthy') is rendered as evidence of his (gendered) stupidity. This 'joke' takes on a poignant tone when Abani informs us that in the original 1980s Nigerian versions, Harry represented the Hausa ethnic group. Humour is a kind of storying, and as Gayatri Spivak's[2] work reminds us, all stories partake in worlding of one kind or another. What stories, then, are embedded in South Africa's recent explosion of negrophobic xenophobia?

'THROW-AWAY' PEOPLE. THESE ARE PEOPLE WHO DO NOT MATTER, WHOSE HUMANITY, ONCE SUCCESSFULLY MISRECOGNISED, RENDERS THEM SAFE TO VIOLATE.

It is necessary to ask questions that chart a path away from the 'incomprehension' which has characterised many South African institutional responses to the xenophobic attacks. Indeed, as I have remarked in other work[3], one of the most dangerous facets of contemporary South African life is the spectre of affected shock at the outbreak of large-scale violence of any sort, from gender-based violence to xenophobic terror. This idiom of uncomprehending shock successfully allows us to disavow agency and complicity in the problems we face. Unless South Africans are an exceedingly naïve nation, it is not possible to be ignorant of how we arrived at a point where Ernesto Nhamuave could be burnt alive for being 'foreign'.

Even a cursory glance at South African society a few years ago would throw up the ways in which, progressive Constitution notwithstanding, there are 'throw-away' people. These are people who do not matter, whose humanity, once successfully misrecognised, renders them safe to violate. Such people range in the South African public eye from poor people of various sorts who can be the nameless 'victims' of violence, farm workers in remote parts of the country and Black lesbians against whom a consistent war is waged, to immigrants from the African continent.

Today the throw-away people we focus on are those deemed 'foreign' because their bodies are marked as such. They can be identified because they are rendered visible – their difference is marked on their bodies, through phenotype. It is this reading of identity as clearly embodied, through pigmentation, that allows for the categorisation of who belongs to South Africa and who not. This bodily badge, codified as 'very darkness', the 'excess' of melanin, hankers after the language of race science, apartheid and white supremacy. Its agents are Black and white. This is an

IT IS NOT SIMPLY XENOPHOBIA, BUT SPECIFICALLY NEGROPHOBIC IN CHARACTER. NO ONE IS ATTACKING WEALTHY FOREIGNERS.

important distinction, no matter how glossed over it was in the media. It is not simply xenophobia, but specifically negrophobic in character. No one is attacking wealthy German, British or French foreigners in Camps Bay or anywhere else in South Africa. European citizens are not among those foreigners who are safe to violate in a xenophobic manner. This is unthinkable.

What makes attacks on some foreigners unthinkable has to do with how sexualised, class marked and racialised South African stories about immigrant communities are. To repeat, what makes it unthinkable is the clear value *and* whiteness of the safe European versus the disposability *and* Blackness of the brutalised African 'foreigner'. The specific racialisation of the attacks matters. This racialisation makes it safe for us to victimise Black people from the African continent in our everyday exchanges, in our legal machinery, through violent Home Affairs practices. It is also coded in how we speak about violence against foreign nationals.

STORY ONE: CRIME

As I listened to Abani, my mind wandered to the stories many South Africans have long told about 'foreign' Africans. Sometimes, these narratives are specific, anchoring to a specific nationality, but with enough flexibility such as the commonly heard assertion: 'All Nigerians are drug-smugglers or criminals of one kind or another. That is why the crime statistics have shot through the roof.' In a context in which South Africans perceive crime as a perpetual problem that the state has failed to curb, 'communities' take it upon themselves to deal with the problem.

Violence against white foreign nationals from Europe and North America is crime and seen as very different from xenophobia, even when they are attacked specifically because they are tourists and therefore read as foreign. Additionally, those from the global north usually have names, personalities, differentiated characteristics/quirks, genders and histories. Their assailants are usually assumed to be young, individual or small groups of nameless Black men, unless caught.

STORY TWO: LANGUAGES OF ENTITLEMENT

Musangi relates widespread reports of how Kikuyu people could be identified in Kenya after they were asked to provide the kiSwahili word for 'orange'. Such categorisation was only possible in a conceptual world which marks Kikuyu people as perpetual mis-pronouncers of words outside their language. A chill ran through my body when I listened to this because of an earlier exchange with a friend who speaks only a peppering of isiSwati as the sole indigenous southern African language he accesses. My friend, whom I will call P, excitedly asked me one evening what the isiZulu word for 'elbow' was. This was linked to an earlier discussion on the popular Gauteng radio station, Yfm, as P drove home.

Puzzled, I nonetheless provided the word, barely used but safely stored in my memory from my high school Zulu first language days. Because people are not in the habit of conducting conversations about their elbows, it is a particularly obscure word. And yet, it is this word that suspected 'foreigners' are expected to produce as proof of their South African identity. This expectation is also coupled with the pejorative labelling of African languages from outside South Africa as incomprehensible. Unlike '*amakwerekwere*', South Africans can speak isiZulu is the underlying belief. It does not matter that South African speakers of other Nguni languages, but who do

IT IS THIS WORD THAT SUSPECTED 'FOREIGNERS' ARE EXPECTED
TO PRODUCE AS PROOF OF THEIR SOUTH AFRICAN IDENTITY.

not also speak isiZulu, would most likely not know the proper word for 'elbow' in isiZulu. Nor does it matter, in this story-world, that Black South Africans speak many other languages, and that many Black South Africans would also not know the word *indololwane*.

This narrative simplifies the marking of South African identity. It is a question reportedly only asked from those read as phenotypically African-Blacks; no coloured-Black or Indian-Black people could be sifted out in this way. It was unthinkable to ask it of white people, nationals or foreign. Indeed, it is possible that this story is an urban legend. Nonetheless, such rumours matter, as Musangi reminds us. Not only does this story reveal something about the markings of insider-outsider status, it also provides information about who the perceived perpetrators are. I will return to the significance of 'Zuluness' as here deployed.

STORY THREE: IMAGINED EMASCULATION

Negrophobic xenophobic sentiment is often couched as a battle between two sets of men. This is very evident in the oft-heard retort: 'These guys come here and steal our women and jobs.' Only the sexual, intimate and romantic preferences of *some* 'foreigners' matter in this way. Such 'foreign' status is not a general, broad, shifting category of non-South Africans. 'Safe' foreigners, protected by race and class privilege, are free of such burdening. Specific masculine entitlement and 'threat' are clearly encoded in this resentful articulation: Black South African women and jobs are the entitlement of Black South African men. Historically as well as in the contemporary moment, dominant Black masculinities index access to finance as linked to sexual attractiveness and virility. Therefore, the loss of both a means of

'THESE GUYS COME HERE AND STEAL OUR WOMEN AND JOBS.'

income and the opposite sex is a threat to such patriarchal and heteronormative masculinities.

The ideological baggage of such assertions comes from assumptions about women's availability for sale. If 'foreign' Africans have all the 'money', then South African men cannot compete, and this becomes the historic rumour which is much touted. Many narratives in the public sphere demonstrate this, but none more consistently than popular model Babalwa Mneno's insistence that she will no longer date South Africans, choosing to focus her romantic interest on African men from elsewhere. The letters pages in the tabloids testify to the specific battles over masculinity that also influence the storying of masculine competition over women and/as resources. It matters that Mneno, as a model, embodies idealised femininity. The story of threat and competition also shows that if women and jobs are a resource and also an entitlement for heterosexual South African men, then the obstacles can be eliminated and indeed must be. This is a bizarre inversion. But then again, inversions always accompany violent epistemic projects.

In a tragic inversion, therefore, immigrants are held responsible for the failure of free market policies to create adequate choices of employment. William Gumede[4] points out that although South Africa's economy has always relied heavily on migrant male labour from the continent, most notably from the neighbouring southern African countries, there is also much anxiety about surplus Black masculine and feminine bodies that cannot immediately be put to profitable use.

Reading Gumede, I was reminded again of how racialised even this is because white foreigners are not really *bodies*, but *minds* in much of the public discourse we generate in South Africa. Were these

THE VICTIMS OF SUCH VIOLENCE BY 'ZULU MOBS' ARE BLEEDING BLACK WOMEN, CRYING BLACK BABIES, BURNING BLACK MEN, SEEN AS 'FOREIGN NATIONALS'.

binaries not so tragic in their material effects, they would be quite boring, given how tidily they invoke Cartesian dualisms. In much of South Africa, white foreign nationals are *assumed* to be useful; they are investors, tourists and the representatives of countries we need to impress with our status as 'world class' or 'emerging nation' – in other words, not like other developing countries.

MOVING TOWARDS SOLUTIONS

Clearly, the idiom around the recent negrophobic attacks has been significantly different. The agents of xenophobic violence are framed repeatedly as 'mobs' of poor Black men in visual and ideological imagery resonant with Inkatha Freedom Party marches/ attacks in townships in past decades under apartheid and the new democracy. Many in news texts and everyday conversations have responded to such imagery as they once did in the 1980s and 1990s: read this imagery to mean 'Zulu men', thereby letting the rest of us off the hook. On the other side, the victims of such violence by 'Zulu mobs' are bleeding Black women, crying Black babies, burning Black men, seen as 'foreign nationals', phrasing which seems the 'nicer' way of saying *amakwerekwere* in English.

These 'mobs' are criminal and out of touch with reality. They have misplaced anger and are out of sync with South African society, we are repeatedly told. Alternatively, they are disgruntled people because of the failure of comprehensive service delivery by the state.

Perhaps there is much value in these stories that explains how we arrived at this frightening place. But then as I leave my office I have to pass several noticeboards on my way out of the building towards the parking lot and my car. Several posters for a bank ask questions such as 'Invest in Ouagadougou? Is that a currency?' The advert only makes sense if we believe in another story, that of non-recognition of African places, cities and references. If Ouagadougou is not recognised as a city in Burkina Faso, then the 'joke' in the advert makes sense. Throughout campus, there are similar adverts for this bank. The place names are mostly African, and they are all in the 'third world'. The 'joke' would not work with New York/Paris/London.

My increasing unease about these posters links to the irresponsibility of such 'jokes' in the interest of capital. They are further supported by a television advert I am forced to watch in which the stereotypical African leader buffoon character is invoked as a figure of parody for a cellular network of which I am a customer. He could be Idi Amin, but he is cast as a character 'type' more so than an historic person in the advert. The 'type' he represents is a stereotype from old colonialist imagery: the African elite as brutal buffoon. The cellular network advertisement, like its bank counterpart, is blatantly racist, and openly negrophobically xenophobic, and in this respect, much like the stories analysed above. Yet there are no 'mobs' of poor 'Zulu' men in my building or home.

Finally, South African institutions, including academic institutions, need to reflect quite critically on the insularity as part of how we, too, have contributed to the violence of past months. For the most part, we continue to be very insular in relation to the scholars, epistemic projects, social and political activity of the rest of our continent. We are not as separate, interestingly, from the intellectual output generated from countries in the north, as Grace Musila[5] has reminded us. We have contributed to the ignorance of the continent we are part of and inadvertently allowed the faceless African man and woman to remain throw-away people.

CONSTRUCTING THE 'OTHER'

LEARNING FROM THE IVORIAN EXAMPLE

VÉRONIQUE TADJO

Many South Africans have expressed shock at the outbreak of xenophobic violence in their country. They thought that they were immune to such nationalist hatred visible elsewhere on the continent (and in the wider world). They believed in the 'rainbow nation' discourse and the specificity of the South African experience. However, as recent events have shown, they were deluding themselves in the same way as less than a decade ago, in my home country of Côte d'Ivoire (Ivory Coast), we did. At the time we thought we were the most peaceful and successful nation in the region – until history taught us otherwise. Reviewing the genesis of the Ivorian crisis might help put in perspective the recent wave of xenophobia that has swept across various townships around South Africa.

As the world's largest producer of cocoa, Côte d'Ivoire used to be West Africa's richest country in per capita terms. It was a magnet for millions of immigrants from poorer neighbouring countries like Burkina Faso, Ghana, Guinea and Mali. They came to work mainly in the coffee and cocoa plantations and to make a better life for themselves. Figures vary, but it is fair to say that at one point in time, these immigrants accounted for up to a third of the Ivorian population.

By the 1990s, the growth rate of the Ivorian economy had slowed to a snail's pace. The model of a liberal economy started to crumble and domestic politics degenerated gradually into crisis. The death in 1993 of Felix Houphouët-Boigny, who had been in power for more than 30 years, was followed by a tense contest for political succession. The collapse of commodity prices on the world market, the huge public debt, unemployment, poverty, widening inequalities between social classes and land scarcity, coupled with financial scandals at the top, brought social unrest and a mounting resentment against 'foreigners'. It was then that Henri Konan Bédié, Houphouët's successor as president, introduced the concept of *Ivoirité*, or Ivorianness.

Houphouët's political power and legitimacy drew upon his Baoule ethnic identity, represented as authentically Ivorian. Ironically, the Baoule are not – even by their own account – indigenous to the region of Côte d'Ivoire, but a people who arrived several hundred years ago from what today would be Ghana. The Baoule believe that in the eighteenth century, Abraha Pokou, an heiress to the Ashanti throne, had to flee into exile after a bloody succession war. She led her partisans through the forest and had to sacrifice her only child in order to save her people. Thus she became the founder of the Baoule kingdom, named after the words *Ba-ou-li* ('the child is dead').[1]

THE MODEL OF A LIBERAL ECONOMY STARTED TO CRUMBLE AND DOMESTIC POLITICS DEGENERATED GRADUALLY INTO CRISIS.

Houphouët relied heavily on the immigrant labour force from neighbouring countries to help develop Côte d'Ivoire, offering them all sorts of economic incentives, including land. Until 1990, they did not need a residence permit and they enjoyed the right to vote. When Bédié came to power after a show of force, he sought to further strengthen the Baoule ethnic identity to which he belonged as well. But he chose to disenfranchise those who were perceived to be non-natives. He bolstered this move by promoting the concept of *Ivoirité*, a concept that implicitly asks the question: who is an Ivorian and who is not? In other words, who are the true Ivorians? This provided a way of defining and securing one's national legitimacy through the stigmatisation of 'foreigners'. It became the basis for affirming the right of the self to belong to the nation while alienating and excluding others.

The promulgation of *Ivoirité* justified political decisions as well as novel cultural practices. Politically, the government prevented opposition leader Alassane Ouattara from contesting presidential elections, on the grounds that his family originally came from Burkina Faso and that he had presented himself as a Burkinabe citizen at one point in his career. (Ouattara, it should be noted, had previously served as prime minister under Houphouët from 1990 to 1993.) Many Muslims who come from the northern part of Côte d'Ivoire, and who had family ties across the border with Burkina Faso, saw this as a sign of their political marginalisation. The tension between the northern and southern regions of Côte d'Ivoire grew deeper and deeper until it reached boiling point. In 2002, civil war broke out when a rebel group took over the north of the country, precipitating a division that persists today.

WHAT CAN SOUTH AFRICANS LEARN FROM THE IVORIAN EXAMPLE?

The rebel New Forces have accused successive govern-ments, including the present one, that of Laurent Gbagbo, of discriminating against northern Muslims and people of foreign origin. In spite of several past peace agreements and the latest Ouagadougou Accord signed in 2007, Côte d'Ivoire remains in effect divided between north and south. Roadblocks are still in place all along the routes that link the two zones. It will be difficult to restore normality in the north among people who have been living for several years without having to pay government taxes, electricity or water bills. Moreover, both sides are trying to maintain control over revenues derived from agricultural exports and mining. Fresh elections are planned for November 30 of this year, amid uncertainty as to whether they will in fact take place.

The concept of *Ivoirité* is at the heart of the crisis. It has undermined national unity, cost hundreds of lives, displaced thousands of people and further weakened the economy. Excluding 'foreigners' is one of the main recurrent methods involved in strategies for conquering or preserving political power, especially when the definition of the 'foreigner' is ambiguous. Being regarded as a 'son or daughter of the soil' brings privileges which are denied to others. In Côte d'Ivoire, this practice was given a legal basis in the 1990s, when residence permits were established and foreigners were banned from entering politics. It is hardly surprising that the issue of identification remains one of the big obstacles on the way to national reunification.

What can South Africans learn from the Ivorian example?

First, they can learn that ethnicity becomes a major threat to social stability when it is manipulated by elite groups driven

by political ambitions. What some of the Ivorian intellectuals did at the instigation of their political leader was to revive the old concept of ethnic classification dating from colonisation in order to mobilise a specific section of society against the 'Others'. One of the architects of the concept of *Ivoirité* wrote:

> *Ivoirité* is like a system whose very coherence requires a closing up of sorts, yes, a closing up ... the closure and control of our borders: to be vigilant about the integrity of one's territory is not xenophobia. Identifying oneself naturally presupposes the differentiation of the 'Other'. And this demarcation implies, whether you like it or not, discrimination. You can't be at the same time yourself and the 'Other'.[2]

Second, South Africans should be wary of blaming xenophobic violence on the unenlightened poor. If the view from outside Côte d'Ivoire was that violence against foreigners seemed to have been solely instigated by the poor, unemployed and uneducated members of the population whose extremist behaviour is to be blamed, the reality is more complex. The Ivorian political leadership actively participated in the exclusion of thousands of foreigners when it saw fit to do so for electoral and economic advantage.

Third, South Africans must recognise that the discourse of 'othering' can always be displaced into other modes of expression. With time, the concept of *Ivoirité* has been reshaped to take on new and more efficient forms. Today, its sphere of influence has shifted from an ethnic dimension to a regional

ETHNICITY BECOMES A MAJOR THREAT TO SOCIAL STABILITY WHEN IT IS MANIPULATED BY ELITE GROUPS DRIVEN BY POLITICAL AMBITIONS.

SOUTH AFRICANS SHOULD BE WARY OF BLAMING XENOPHOBIC VIOLENCE ON **THE UNENLIGHTENED POOR.**

one. The notion of the 'foreigner' has become dual. The 'Other' is not just the one who doesn't belong to the national territory. The 'Other' has also become the one who is not from the local territory. Ivorians from the south feel they have little in common with 'these Muslims', 'these traders' and 'these foreigners' from up north. Ivorians from the north have in turn acquired a greater cultural, religious and political awareness.

And in an even more complex turn of events, regionalism has taken an added dimension, especially in the western agricultural areas where the land issue is particularly critical. People known in Côte d'Ivoire as *allogènes* (nationals who have moved from the area where they were born to another one) are treated like foreigners, particularly in disputes over their exploitation of local natural resources. Violence perpetrated by *autochthones* (nationals from the area) can become a means to exclude *allogènes* or to repossess their assets.

Fourth, South Africans must retain a critical awareness of the historical – and, in particular, the colonial – roots of current conflicts. The Ivorian crisis can be viewed, in part, as a consequence of the borders inherited from colonisation. When Africa was carved up the colonialists did not take into account religious and cultural affiliations. South Africa is no exception to the rule, and bears the added historical memory of governance by racial and ethnic division under apartheid.

It is true that France, the erstwhile colonial power in Côte d'Ivoire, has played a much more active role in intervening in that country's crisis than foreign powers have in South Africa. France has retained a military base and a strong economic influence in the country since independence. The CFA franc – the

SOUTH AFRICANS MUST RETAIN A CRITICAL AWARENESS OF THE HISTORICAL – AND, IN PARTICULAR, THE COLONIAL – ROOTS OF CURRENT CONFLICTS.

national currency – is linked to the Euro. French troops are seen by the government side and at times by the former rebels as a force which is interfering in an internal conflict. Nevertheless, France will remain as one of the key players in the return to peace because of its continuous political sphere of influence.

Finally, South Africans will need to recognise that, just as in the Côte d'Ivoire, the lack of a consistent immigration policy in the context of an economy in which the majority of the population still has only marginal access to a secure livelihood has proven a recipe for disaster. Political identity comes with borders. The idea of the nation-state as a well-defined entity demands the protection of its borders. The perceived threat of invasion by immigrants leads to the use of repression both within the boundaries of the national community and against those identified as outsiders. At the grass-roots level, xenophobia can be fuelled by opportunism and the desire to get quick material gains from driving away foreigners.

The South African authorities must now act decisively to decrease the flow of immigration from all over the continent and from neighbouring countries like Zimbabwe and Mozambique in particular. At the same time they must work harder at integrating the immigrant population which is already present in its territory. The perpetrators of violence must be put on trial. Justice needs to be done and seen to be done. Maintaining a state of impunity would only prepare the ground for renewed attacks, especially considering the fact that South Africa is a society that already has a history of violence. The probability of xenophobia taking on other forms of expression at a time of tense political competition should not be under-estimated.

The possibility that South Africa might see its recent experience reflected in that of other African states is undermined by the persistence of ignorance. With the end of apartheid, South Africa has opened up to the outside world. Unfortunately, in the collective imagination, the rest of Africa is still an unknown reality laden with negative associations. Not enough has been done to counter this ignorance. At times, the media, instead of fulfilling its central obligation to educate and inform, reproduces clichés. The *Daily Sun* has been blamed for such excesses. Its coverage of the xenophobic violence has been seen as biased and inflammatory. But this is also our own fault. We Africans are not talking to one another. The difficulty of travelling inside the African continent, unworkable currency exchanges, linguistic barriers and the age-old divide between Francophones, Anglophones and Lusophones are all factors that have turned us into strangers living side by side.

We need to think about borders differently. Look at Europe, which is redefining its territorial space in the process of deciding how far it can go in being multicultural. Economies like those of the United States have developed thanks to immigrants. Barack Obama, one of their presidential candidates, had a Kenyan father.

South Africa's transformation cannot happen in a vacuum. Poverty is not measured in financial terms only. Poverty comes when one loses one's creativity and potential for change. It is befitting in this context, and in conclusion, to quote Albert Camus, the French/Algerian writer who won the Nobel Prize in 1957 and who was known for his great humanism:

Each generation doubtless feels called upon to reform the world. Mine knows that it will not reform it, but its task is perhaps even greater. It consists in preventing the world from destroying itself. Heir to a corrupt history, in which are mingled fallen revolutions, technology gone mad, dead gods, and worn-out ideologies, where mediocre powers can destroy all yet no longer know how to convince, where intelligence has debased itself to become the servant of hatred and oppression, this generation starting from its own negations will have to re-establish, both within and without, a little of that which constitutes the dignity of life and death. [3]

END NOTES

INTRODUCTION

1   27 May 2008. http://www.spiegel.de/international/world/
    0,1518,555821,00.html.

2   As Owen Sichone observes, both the form and the explicit
    motivation behind the xenophobic violence of May 2008 were already
    found in the year of the transition to democracy. Beginning late in
    1994, a pogrom labeled *buyelekhaya* ('go back home') unfolded over
    a period of several weeks in Alexandra township, wherein gangs
    of youth claiming membership in the African National Congress,
    the South African Communist Party and the South African National
    Civic Organisation sought to drive out 'undocumented workers'. See
    Sichone, 2008. 'Xenophobia' . In N Shepherd and S Robins (eds.),
    New South African Keywords. Johannesburg and Athens: Jacana and
    Ohio University Press, p. 256.

3   See Anton Harber's contribution to this volume. John and Jean
    Comaroff have tracked how the discourse of an 'alien invasion'
    – applied equally to exogenous plant species and to immigrant
    humans – has registered widespread anxiety around sovereignty
    and national security in the years immediately following the end
    of apartheid and the relaxation of border controls. Jean Comaroff
    and John L Comaroff. 2001. 'Naturing the Nation: Aliens,
    Apocalypse and the Postcolonial State'. *Journal of Southern
    African Studies.* 27, 3 (2001): 627-651.

4   The survey was conducted by Futurefact. See Janine Erasmus,
    'SA still upbeat about the Future'. MediaClubSouthAfrica.com
    15 July 2008. http://www.mediaclubsouthafrica.com/index.

php?option=com_content&view=article&id=567:futurefact-survey-
2007-150708&catid=42:land_news&Itemid=51.

5   http://www.aprm.org.za/docs/SACountryReviewReport5.pdf,
    accessed 31 August 2008. See in particular chapter 7.1.10, 'Racism
    and Xenophobia'.

6   Address of the President of South Africa, Thabo Mbeki, at the
    National Tribute in remembrance of the victims of attacks on foreign
    nationals, 3 July 2008. Tshwane. http://www.thepresidency.gov.za/
    show.asp?type=sp&include=president/sp/2008/sp07031559.htm.

7   They constitute what Jacques Derrida might think of as the
    'constitutive outside' of the category of the citizen. See Judith
    Butler, 'Contingent Foundations: Feminism and the Question of
    the Postmodern', in Seyla Benhabib et al, *Feminist Contentions: A
    Philosophical Exchange.* New York: Routledge, 1995.

8   See the contributions by Loren Landau and Andile Mngxitama to
    this volume.

9   As Achille Mbembe remarked at our colloquium.

10 The Book of Judges (Chapter 12) tells the story of how the
    Gileadites used the pronunciation of the word *shibboleth* as a test
    to expose and kill Ephraimites who were trying to surreptitiously
    cross the Jordan river back into their conquered homeland. The
    language of the Ephraimites had no /sh/ sound. See: http://
    en.wikipedia.org/wiki/Shibboleth.

11 See the film *Affectionately Known as Alex*, by Danny Turken
    (Filmmakers Against Racism, 2008).

12 For a richly perceptive discussion of the tension between inherited
    racial classifications and lived racial identities in the post-
    apartheid era, see Zimitri Erasmus, 'Race and Identity in the
    Nation', in A Habib, R Southall, J Daniel and J Lutchmann (eds.),
    The State of the Nation: 2004-2005. Pretoria: HSRC Press, pp. 9-35.

13 *The Star*, 25 June 2008.

14 Appadurai, A. 'Dead Certainty: Ethnic Violence in the Era of Globalization', *Public Culture* 10(2), (Winter 1998), pp. 225-247. Véronique Tadjo, in her contribution to this volume, suggests that South Africans would do well to educate themselves about other African cases, notably Côte d'Ivoire, where the identification and disenfranchisement of 'foreigners' within the 'authentic nation' has fomented civil war.

15 See Achille Mbembe, 'If only we could live without borders', *Sunday Tribune*, 15 June 2008.

16 Although as post-graduate student leader Charles Nyuykonge pointed out in his presentation to the colloquium, Wits University itself actively discriminates against foreign students who are not from the Southern African Development Community through the imposition of a substantial supplementary fee.

CHAPTER 2 – I DID NOT EXPECT SUCH A THING TO HAPPEN

1   Rolf Maruping's story was recorded by Phefumula Nyoni as part of the Wits Forced Migration Studies Programme's 'Documenting Experiences of Xenophobic Violence Study'. See http://www.migration.org.za. The interview was conducted at the Rand Airport shelter.

CHAPTER 4 – XENOPHOBIA IN ALEXANDRA

1   *City Vision*. 11-17 June 2008.

2   'Alexandra Benchmark Survey'. 2005.

3   *City Vision*. 11-17 June 2008.

4   Baskin, J. 2007. 'Alexandra Renewal Project Strategic Review'. March 2007.

5   *The Star*. 22 January 2001.

6   *Alex News*. 15-28 May 2008.

7   *The Star*. 15 December 2000.

8   Interview with Matome Rasetelo, 24 June 2008.

CHAPTER 5 – BEHIND XENOPHOBIA IN SOUTH AFRICA – POVERTY OR INEQUALITY?

1   This is equivalent to R430 in 2006 prices, close to the means test threshold for old age pension recipients of R454. P Armstrong, B Lekezwa & K Siebrits. 2008. 'Poverty in South Africa: A Profile Based on Recent Household Surveys'. *Stellenbosch Economic Working Papers* 04/08, citing data from the *StatsSA Income and Expenditure Survey 2005*.

2   Woolard, I & Leibbrandt, M. 2006. 'Towards a Poverty Line for South Africa: Background Note'. Southern Africa Labour and Development Research Unit, University of Cape Town.

3   The Gini coefficient is a measure of inequality which varies between 0 to indicate complete equality and 1 to indicate complete inequality. The estimate of 0.73 is based on individuals rather than households, and takes account of income from work and social security grants. See StatsSA (2008), *Income and Expenditure of Households 2005/6: Analysis of results*, Report no. 01-00-01, Table 17.

4   All data in this paragraph are from StatsSA (2008), ibid.

5   National Treasury. 2008. *2008 Budget Review,* pp. 95-96.

6   StatsSA (2008), ibid.

7   Van der Berg, S & Burger, R. 2003. 'Education and Socio-Economic Differentials: A Study of School Performance in the Western Cape'. *SA Journal of Economics,* 71: 3.

8   Human Rights Commission. 2003. *Fourth Annual Economic and*

Social Rights Report: 2000–2002, Johannesburg.

9   Rust, K. 2003. 'No Shortcuts to Progress: South Africa's Progress in Implementing its Housing Policy, 1994-2002'. Institute for Housing in SA, Johannesburg; LN Sisulu. Department of Housing Budget Vote 2008/9. 28 May 2008. National Assembly, Cape Town.

CHAPTER 6 – RELATIVE DEPRIVATION, SOCIAL INSTABILITY AND CULTURES OF ENTITLEMENT

1   A comment by a male caller to a Radio 702 talk show in July 2008.

2   *Business Day.* 24 July 2006.

3   *Business Day.* 14 July 2008. To be fair, Bruce made this point in the context of arguing that because there were so many politicians looting, it would cause too much political instability if we were to seek justice against all of them. This, however, does not detract from the main thrust of his comment, which is about preserving the system of accumulation and inequality.

4   *The Times.* 23 June 2005. (This comment was made in 1996.)

5   The South African Communist Party (SACP) first used this term in a 2006 discussion document to mark the appearance of the economically orthodox Growth, Employment and Redistribution macro-economic strategy in 1996.

6   Ironically backed, with enthusiasm, by the SACP and the Congress of South African Trade Unions leadership. Working class leadership or leading the working class like sheep to the slaughter?

7   Gramsci, A. 1971. *Selections from Prison Notebooks.* London: Lawrence & Wishart, p. 276.

8   Sachs, W. 1999. *Planet Dialectics: Explorations in Environment*

and Development. London: Zed. See also Wolfgang Sachs (ed). 2002. 'The Jo'burg Memo: Memorandum for the World Summit on Sustainable Development'. Johannesburg: Heinrich Boll Foundation.

CHAPTER 7 – VIOLENCE, CONDEMNATION, AND THE MEANING OF LIVING IN SOUTH AFRICA

1   'Legal group condemns Itireleng arrests'. 22 February 2008. *Cape Times*. Online at http://www.capetimes.co.za/?fSectionI d=&fArticleId=nw20080221231957529C634536# (accessed 24 February 2008).

2   Quotation is from an address on Africa Day (25 May 2008). Online at http://www.info.gov.za/speeches/2008/08052608451001.htm (accessed 27 June 2008).

3   Minister of Safety and Security Charles Nqakula initially responded to the attacks in Alexandra by claiming, 'It is only a problem, but if it were a crisis, it would be happening right across the country'. *Pretoria News*, 14 May 2008.

4   In a South African government statement condemning the attacks, Minister of Home Affairs Nosiviwe Mapisa-Nqakula wrote that, 'The picture is that foreigners are under siege, but the fact is that criminal elements are clean-sweeping everybody in the community' (in 'Govt slams xenophobic attacks'. *South Africa Info*, 16 May 2008. http://www.southafrica.info/about/ democracy/xenophobia-160508.htm (accessed 26 May 2008). See also 'ANC: Sinister forces at work'. *News 24*. 14 May 2008. http://www.news24.com/News24/South_Africa/News/0,,2-7-1442_2322013,00.html (accessed 22 May 2008).

5   Consortium for Refugees and Migrants in South Africa. 2008.

'Protecting Refugees, Asylum Seekers, and Immigrants in South Africa'. Johannesburg: Consortium for Refugees and Migrants in South Africa (online at www.cormsa.org.za).

6   See, for example, the response to Raymond Suttner's criticisms by South African Communist Party spokesman Malesela Maleka in *Business Day*, 4 May 2006. Online at http://www.businessday.co.za/articles/article.aspx?ID=BD4A194585 (accessed 15 July 2008).

7   Nevin, T. 2006. 'New Club Triggers Race Tensions'. *African Business*, August/September; 'South Africa: Landau and Race', *Business Day* (5 September 2007). Media 24. See also 'Zuma OK with "no whites" rule, Online at http://www.news24.com/News24/South_Africa/Politics/0,,2-7-12_2275834,00.html (accessed 24 June 2008).

8   See statement by the South African Institute of Race Relations on causal factors behind the violent unrest in and around Johannesburg, 20 May 2008. Online at http://www.sairr.org.za/press-office/archive/statement-by-the-south-african-institute-of-race-relations-on-causal-factors-behind-the-violent-unrest-in-and-around-johannesburg-20-may-2008.html (accessed 8 June 08). See also Human Sciences Research Council. 2008. *Citizenship, Violence and Xenophobia in South Africa: Perceptions from South African Communities*. Human Science Research Council: Pretoria. Cilliers, Jakkie. 2008. 'Xenophobia, Conspiracies and the Absence of Leadership'. 20 May 2008. Online at http://www.issafrica.org/index.php?link_id=4059&slink_id=5959&link_type=12&slink_type=12&tmpl_id=3 (accessed 9 June 2008). For indication of the Democratic Alliance position, see 'Zille warns against opening of borders', in which the Democratic Alliance leader is quoted as, 'The recent wave of xenophobic attacks is a direct result of the government's failure to properly control immigration into South

Africa'. *Mail and Guardian Online*. 27 May 2008. Online at http://
ww2.mg.co.za/article/2008-05-27-zille-warns-against-opening-of-
borders (accessed 17 June 2008).

9   Landau, L B. 2006. 'Transplants and Transients: Idioms of
Belonging and Dislocation in Inner-City Johannesburg'. *African
Studies Review*, Vol 49(2): pp. 125-145.

CHAPTER 8 – CROSSING BORDERS

1   *Sunday Independent*. 25 May 2008. 'An old plague rises to the
surface'. p. 13.

2   Dr James made this argument in his recent participation in
a debate, 'Never Again: A Debate on Xenophobia', held at the
University of the Witwatersrand on 17 June 2008.

3   Home Affairs officials refer to the police teams whose 'special
assignment' it is to conduct sweeps searching for illegal
immigrants as 'border police'.

CHAPTER 9 – POLICING XENOPHOBIA – XENOPHOBIC POLICING: A CLASH OF LEGITIMACY

1   'Legal group condemns Itireleng arrests'. Published on the Web by
IOL on 22 February 2008. http://www.iol.co.za.

2   I would like to thank Caroline Wanjiku Kihato for relating this story
to me and allowing me to use it for the purpose of this essay.

CHAPTER 10 – HOUSING DELIVERY, THE URBAN CRISIS AND XENOPHOBIA

1   Some statistics drawn from the 2001 population census illustrate
this increasing mobility, for example. At that time 11 per cent
of Johannesburg's citizens had lived in the city for fewer than
five years, and 5.4 per cent of the population were foreign-born.

These figures are likely to have increased.

2   State-subsidised houses that were seen as part of the Reconstruction and Development Programme inaugurated by the government in 1994.

3   The standard unit and plot conformed largely to the norms and standards required by the Housing Act, 1997 (Act 107 of 1997), namely a 250m^2 plot with a house of no less than 30m^2. The subsidy amount was initially R15 000 and it has progressively increased to the current level of some R43 500 for the top structure (now required to be at least 40m^2).

4   This prohibition period was recently reduced from an eight-year period.

5   It is a bizarre anomaly that beneficiaries must earn more to access rental housing than freehold housing.

6   http://www.joburg.org.za/content/view/2574/168/

7   Huchzermeyer, M. '2008. Slums law based on flawed interpretation of UN goals'. *Business Day*. 19 May 2008.

8   The authors conducted detailed research into land management practices in Hillbrow in early 2007 as part of a project commissioned by Planact and the Centre for Urban and Built Environment Studies, a research unit in the School of Architecture and Planning. Data on Hillbrow is derived from this report.

9   'State of the Cities Report'. 2006. South African Cities Network, pp. 2-27.

10 The suggested new approach is informed by Jennifer Robinson's theorisation of the 'ordinary city'. This emphasises the importance of local spaces – social as well as economic – and the need to strengthen the position of informal as well as formal enterprises.

CHAPTER 11 – TWO NEWSPAPERS, TWO NATIONS? THE MEDIA

AND THE XENOPHOBIC VIOLENCE

1   It was not the only paper to use 'alien', though most media stopped using it when it was removed from the statute book a few years ago as the official designation. The *Sowetan* was still occasionally using it, but the *Daily Sun* was the last to persist and to do it with such consistency and relish.

2   *The Star.* 4 April 2008.

CHAPTER 12 – BEYOND CITIZENSHIP: HUMAN RIGHTS AND DEMOCRACY

1   S v Makwanyane per Mahomed J 1995 (3) SA 391 (CC); 1995 (6) BCLR 665 para 262.

2   Preamble, Constitution of the Republic of South Africa, Act 108 of 1996. The 1993 (Interim) Constitution (Constitution of the Republic of South Africa, Act 200 of 1993) was the product of the political negotiations of the early 1990s. This was succeeded, in 1997, by the 1996 Constitution which was drafted by the first democratic Parliament sitting as the Constitutional Assembly.

3   S v Makwanyane per Mokgoro J para 308. (Footnotes omitted.)

4   1998 (1) SA 245 (CC); 1997 (12) BCLR 1655 (CC).

5   Larbi-Odam para 19.

6   Para 31.

7   Paras 25 & 38.

8   Minister of Home Affairs v Watchenuka 2004 (4) SA 326 (SCA) para 25.

9   2004 (6) SA 505 (CC), (2004) 6 BCLR 569 (CC).

10 2007 (4) SA 395 (CC).

11 Para 28.

12 Para 122.

13 Para 122.

CHAPTER 13 – WE ARE NOT ALL LIKE THAT

1   Chinweizu. 'On Negrophobia: Psychoneurotic Obstacles to Black Autonomy (or Why I just love Michael Jackson)'. www.africawithin. com/chinweizu/on_negrophobia.htm.

2   Biko, S. 1978. *I Write What I Like*. Bowerden Press. Reprinted 2004 by Picador Africa.

3   Clark, DJ, Fage, JD, Oliver, R A & Roberts, AD. 1975. *The Cambridge History of Africa*. Cambridge University Press, p. 463.

4   Fromm, E. 1991. *Marx's Concept of Man*. New York: Continuum, p. 206.

5   Fanon, F. 1967. *Black Skins White Masks*. New York: Grove Press, p.11.

6   Fanon, F. ibid, p. 12.

7   Biko, S. 1978. *I Write What I Like*. Bowerden Press. Reprinted 2004 by Picador Africa.

CHAPTER 14 – BRUTAL INHERITANCES: ECHOES, NEGROPHOBIA AND MASCULINIST VIOLENCE

1   TED, founded in 1984, stands for Technology, Entertainment, Design, and was started as an endeavour to bring people from those fields into conversation with one another on public platforms. Since then, TED and TEDGlobal conferences try to bring together 'the world's most fascinating thinkers and doers, who are challenged to give the talk of their lives'. Abani's talk was presented at the 2nd TEDGlobal conference.

2   Spivak, GC. 1996. 'Bonding in Difference' (with Alfred Arteaga), in Donna Landry and Gerald Maclean (eds). *The Spivak Reader*. New York & London: Routledge.

    _. 1985. 'Three Women's Texts and a Critique of Imperialism'. *Critical Inquiry*, 12 (Autumn).

3   Gqola, PD. 2007. 'How the "cult of femininity" and violent masculinities support endemic gender-based violence in contemporary South Africa'. *African Identities*, 2007, 5.1: pp. 111-124.

4   Gumede, W. 2008. 'Failing its people'. Guardian.co.uk, 20 May 2008, archived at http://commentisfree.guardian.co.uk/william_gumede/2008/05/failing_its_people.html, accessed on 28 May 2008.

5   Musila, G. 2008. 'Lot's Wife's Backward Glance and Zola 7 in Africa: The South Africa-Africa Dis/connect in Literary Studies'. Paper presented at the symposium 'South African Literary Studies: A Provocation on the State of the Field'. 16-17 April. University of the Witwatersrand, Johannesburg.

CHAPTER 15 – CONSTRUCTING THE 'OTHER': LEARNING FROM THE IVORIAN EXAMPLE

1   Houphouët-Boigny, F. 1994. *Mes Premiers Combats*. Nouvelles Editions Ivoiriennes/ Edition 1, Abidjan/Paris.

2   Jolivet, E. 2002-3. Section Service Public, Séminaire: 'Le Fait National l'Ivoirité. De la Conceptualisation à la Manipulation de l'Identité Ivoirienne'. Author's translation.

3   Albert Camus' speech at the Nobel banquet at the City Hall in Stockholm, 10 December 1957.

OTHER SOURCES :

Duval, P. 2003. *Fantômes d'Ivoire.* Editions du Rocher, Paris.

Touré, A. 1981. *La Civilisation Quotidienne en Côte d'Ivoire.* Editions Karthala, Paris.

AUTHOR BIOGRAPHIES

Cathi Albertyn is a professor in the School of Law at the University of the Witwatersrand, Johannesburg (hereafter, Wits University). She is a constitutional law and human rights specialist with a particular interest in equality, gender and the law, and the role of constitutional rights in securing social and economic justice. She is co-editor (with Elsje Bonthuys) of *Gender, Law and Justice* (2007).

David B Coplan is professor of Anthropology at Wits University. He has been researching and writing about issues of migration and borders in southern Africa, with a particular focus on Lesotho and South Africa, for 15 years. His other publications in the field include: *In the Time of Cannibals: Word Music of South Africa's Basotho Migrants* (1994); 'Passport Control Reform at the Free State – Lesotho International Border' 2001; *The Border Within: The Future of the Lesotho-South African International Boundary* 2002; *Lice in Your Blanket: The Meaning of the Lesotho-Free State Border* (2000); 'A River Runs Through It: The Meaning of The Lesotho-Free State Border' (2001); *A Measure of Civilisation: Revisiting the Caledon Valley Frontier* (2000); and 'Unconquered Territory: Narrating the Caledon Valley' (2000).

Alex Eliseev has been a reporter for *The Star* newspaper since 2005. He has also worked for the *Sunday Times*, the South African Press Association (Sapa) and Caxton. He immigrated to South Africa from Russia in 1991 and covered the May 2008 xenophobic attacks extensively.

Stephen Gelb is a political economist at Wits University and executive director of The EDGE Institute in Johannesburg. He has taught in Canada, the United States and South Africa and worked as a policy adviser for the African National Congress and several government departments after 1994. He is widely published on South African economic and political issues. His current research interests are inequality and growth, and the role of foreign direct investment in development in a range of countries including India, Kenya and South Africa.

Daryl Glaser is an associate professor of Political Studies at the University of the Witwatersrand. He formerly taught at the University of Strathclyde, Glasgow. His main interests are in normative political theory and South Africa. He is the author of *Politics and Society in South Africa* (2001) and co-editor of *Twentieth Century Marxism: A Global Introduction* (2007).

Pumla Dineo Gqola is a feminist scholar, writer and blogger, who holds a DPhil in postcolonial studies from the University of Munich. She is associate professor of Literary, Cultural and Media Studies at the University of the Witwatersrand, and has published widely on slave memory, sexualities, African feminisms and gendered Blackness. Her co-edited projects include *Discourses on Difference, Discourses on Oppression* and *I Like What I Write: A Collection of Essays Inspired by the Writings of Steve Biko* (2008).

Anton Harber is the Caxton professor of Journalism and Media Studies at Wits University. He was the co-founder and co-editor of the *Weekly Mail* (now the *Mail & Guardian*) and was editor of both the first and second editions of *The A–Z of South African Politics*. He was an executive producer of the television series *Ordinary People* and *Hard Copy*. A recipient of the Pringle Award for Press Freedom and the Missouri Medal of Honour, Harber writes a column in *Business Day* and a blog at www.theharbinger.co.za.

Shireen Hassim is associate professor of Political Studies at the University of the Witwatersrand. She is the author of *Women's Organizations and Democracy in South Africa: Contesting Authority* (2006), which won the 2007 American Political Science Association's Victoria Shuck Award for best book on women and politics. She co-edited, with Anne Marie Goetz, *No Shortcuts to Power: African Women in Politics and Policy-Making* (2003), and with Shahra Razavi, *Gender and Social Policy in Global Context: Uncovering the Gendered Structure of the 'Social'* (2006).

Julia Hornberger, PhD, was a doctoral fellow at WISER and is now an assistant professor in the Department of Anthropology of the University of Zurich, Switzerland. Her research deals with issues of community policing, private policing, violence and human rights, crime, and issues of the state, urban governance and migration in Johannesburg. Her doctoral thesis is entitled 'Don't Push this Constitution Down my Throat! Human Rights in Everyday Practice. An Ethnography of Police Transformation in Johannesburg, South Africa'. The thesis is an ethnographic account of everyday policing in Johannesburg caught between the unprecedented legitimacy of human rights in the political life of early post-1994 South Africa and societal practices of informal and popular justice.

Tawana Kupe is Dean of the Faculty of Humanities and associate professor of Media Studies at Wits University. He is a columnist for *City Press* newspaper, *Maverick* and *Empire* magazines, and a frequent commentator on radio and television. He is chairperson of the board of the Media Monitoring Project and editor of *Broadcasting Policy and Practice in Africa* (2003).

Loren B Landau is director of the Forced Migration Studies Programme at Wits University (www.migration.org.za). He is a political scientist by training; his research explores migration, sovereignty, and belonging in South and Eastern Africa. Author of *The Humanitarian Hangover: Displacement, Aid and Transformation in Western Tanzania* (2008), he has published widely in academic and policy-oriented journals and reports. He is also currently the executive committee chair for the Consortium of Refugees and Migrants in South Africa (CoRMSA).

Rolf Maruping is an electrical repairman who is passionate about music and hopes to start his own band. He was born in South Africa to Mozambican parents. He has lived in Johannesburg all his life. The main breadwinner in his extended family, Maruping was interviewed while sheltering from the violence at the Rand Airport, having lost all his possessions. Despite his experiences in May and June 2008, he is committed to remaining in South Africa as it is home.

Andile Mngxitama is a recipient of the Ford International Scholarship and is a doctoral student at Wits University. He is the co-editor of *Biko Lives! The Contested Legacies of Steve Biko* (2008), and an activist in the Landless People's Movement. He is also an associate of the Institute of Black Studies.

Noor Nieftagodien is a senior researcher in the National Research Foundation programme 'Local Pasts, Current Realities' and is a senior lecturer in History at Wits University, where he teaches courses in urban history and African cities. He is also the deputy head of the History Workshop. His research interests include township histories, urban restructuring and local social movements. Noor has co-authored with Phil Bonner, *Kathorus – A History*. Their latest work, *Alexandra - A History*, will be published in November 2008.

Devan Pillay is head of Sociology at Wits University, and formerly a government official, a trade unionist with the National Union of Mineworkers, director of the Social Policy Programme at the University of Durban-Westville, editor of the journal *Work In Progress* and staff writer for the *SA Labour Bulletin*. He was active in the anti-apartheid movement, and served time in prison for furthering the aims of the African National Congress.

Melinda Silverman is an urban development specialist. She was editor-in-chief of the *State of Cities Report 2006*. She is also a practising urban designer and lecturer in the School of Architecture and Planning, Wits University. She writes about cities in both popular and academic publications and has co-authored a series of articles in the *Mail & Guardian* on urban life. These stories, based on interviews with ordinary people, have documented at first hand some of the conflicts that characterise the contemporary city in South Africa. She has a special interest in exploring the intersections between urban informality and modernist practices.

Alon Skuy graduated as a photographer from the Market Photo Workshop in 2005. Since then he has worked as a freelance photographer for several for several newspapers and is now working at *The Times*. He is the winner of the 2008 Mondi Shanduka Newspaper Award for his photograph Hillbrow Flight. He is the 2008 Ruth First Fellow and presented an exhibition of 26 extraordinary photographs, entitled *Inside the Bridge*. These photographs depicted the lives of a community of people who live inside a Johannesburg concrete highway bridge.

Véronique Tadjo is a senior lecturer and the head of French Studies in the School of Literature and Language Studies, Wits University. She is also a writer and a painter. She holds a BA from the University of Abidjan in Côte d'Ivoire, her country of origin, and a doctorate from the Sorbonne, Paris. Selected titles in English: *As The Crow Flies*, Heinemann (2001); *The Shadow of Imana: Travels to the Heart of Rwanda*, Heinemann (2002); *Red Earth: Poems*, Eastern Washington University Press (2006), and *The Blind Kingdom*, Ayebia Clarke Publishing (2008).

Eric Worby joined Wits University as professor and head of the School of Social Sciences in 2006 after teaching for ten years in the Department of Anthropology at Yale University. His research and publications have been concerned with agrarian transformation, modernity, sovereignty, public culture, the state and ethnicity, primarily in northwestern Zimbabwe but also in Botswana, Tanzania, South Africa and Bangladesh.

Tanya Zack is a town planner. The focus of her research and practice is on housing and urban poverty. She has most recently been involved in the writing of best practice case studies, an evaluation of urban renewal projects, and research into inner city land use management, the development of sustainable human settlements and urban public investment to promote the inclusion of poor and marginalised residents in South African cities.